Welcome to My Front Porch

365 Days of Inspiration

Molly Dillor

D1603863

Metastudies Inst.
Corona, CA

To Kate
Love + Blessings!
Molly Dillon

Permission to quote from the following sources granted by:

Dedication

I dedicate this book to:
Common Ground Spiritual Center, Corona CA
and
Common Ground Spiritual Center, Tustin CA

Acknowledgements

Where do I begin? So many loving souls—so many!

To my children, my step-children, my adopted children, my grand-children and my great-grandchildren: You are loved to the moon and back.

For those of you who allowed me to use your lovely poetry and your inspiring quotes, thank you! Each of your contributions helped to make my book a beautiful symphony.

This manuscript could not have been birthed without the 'midwife-ry' assistance of my fabulous writers' critique group, Mondays at Molly's: Carol J. Amato, Amanda Ashley, Stephanie Jefferson, Judith McAllister, and Mart Shaughnessy.

To Metastudies Inst. and Anita Burns for having such profound belief in this book that you were willing to take this awesome journey with me. Thank you.

And, most of all, I am so very grateful to my husband, Bill, for his hours of research and his endearing faith. I love you!

Welcome to My Front Porch

365 Days of Inspiration

Welcome to My Front Porch

Introduction

In writing this book, I have jotted down inspired thoughts gained while sitting on my front porch or in my humble sanctuary—and, even sometimes, from under the umbrella of my favorite sidewalk café. At the age of 76, I have been privileged to lead many lives and taken numerous spiritual paths.

I am not one to put a name to my beliefs; I simply sit and open up to the Universe, waiting in silence to gain insights and ideas. Like the Dalai Lama, I merely want to come from love. Is there another place from which any of us can truly emerge? I think not.

For you, my readers, I want this book to be a daily sample of spiritual nectar. I ask that you sip from this bound bird feeder like the red-throated hummingbirds do from the glass feeder on my front porch.

When referring to God, I often call Him/Her by different names. I love thinking of God as the Beloved, but at other times I might picture Him as the Divine, or maybe, Her, as Infinite Love. I also refer to God in both the masculine and feminine gender. I remember, as a child, we had a minister in our church who always ended the service with this benediction, "May the Mother love of the Father God go with you." Isn't that beautiful?

Where my naming of God does not resonate with you, please substitute your own name for Him/Her—one that better suits your own spiritual path.

Through this endeavor, I want you to know who I am, to get the feel of my spirit, to see how I dance and sing in this world. No matter where or how we worship, we are all, every one of us, soul-connected and each has something important to share with the other. My desire is to reach out and touch you as though the two of us were sitting together in quiet conversation.

At the end of each chat, I say "NAMASTE," a salutation that is a Sanskrit term meaning "The Divine in me greets the Divine in you."

The day I initiated this venture, I bowed my head and asked the Great Co-Creator to guide me. I jotted that prayer down and have been repeating it each day before I begin my writing:

Be a giant, snow-white Egret, my Beloved.

Let me sit upon your feathered back

While you fly me to places within my heart that I never knew existed.

Take me wherever you need me to go

That I might impart our Magical journeys to others.

Co-create with me a benediction of love.

NAMASTE

January 1

Angels and Buddhas

"Avoid what is evil; do what is good; purify the mind—this is the
teaching of the Awakened One (Buddha)
-Suttapitaka. Dhammapada, 14:183

"He shall give his angels charge over thee, to keep thee in all thy ways."
-Psalm 11:13

This morning I rest on my front porch in the quiet, yawning dawn of a
new year. My eyes wander aimlessly to a table positioned between two
cushioned patio chairs. The base of the table is concrete, the shape of a
sleeping angel. A piece of circular glass rests on its head and wings. A
figure of a meditating Buddha perches on top of this angelic table—a
double dose of spirituality.

Lying beside me, my three-pound miniature Pomeranian, Punkie,
stares at the Buddha in open-eyed meditation. This human fur ball has
practiced the art of meditation for most of her fifteen years. She goes so
deep that the world could collapse around her and she'd still be breathing
out a long, sighing "Ohmmmm." (At least that's what I like to think.)

I reach out and stroke my small companion and then, closing my
eyes, I hear these words:
I am, as Buddha, sitting under the Bodhi Tree,
Contemplating my holy state.
I am wisdom, knowing all things without knowing that I know,
Believing in a perfect way without wholly understanding that way.
I am traveling toward the next plane—that perfect journey back home

And, as I travel, I co-create with the Beloved whom I have never seen.

That Loving Force that whispers thoughts and ideas into my ear if I but listen,

That One who lives within me—as me. The Great I Am.

-Author

Affirmation: With welcoming arms, I embrace my spirituality.

NAMASTE

January 2

Our Lives are Always Perfect

"Everything by an impulse of its own nature tends towards its
perfection."
-Dante

I have lived through seventy-six changings of the seasons; trudged through two divorces and the death of my third husband; almost died at my birth when a nurse brought into the hospital nursery a disease that small immune systems could not fight off. For weeks, I lay in the hospital fighting for my life. And, believe it or not, it was all perfect—my life is and always will be PERFECT.

At present, I am in a twenty-five-year-marriage that, like the passion fruit vines growing from either side of my garden arbor, has intermingled; ripening and blending with time. (I love these particular "it is all perfect" years.)

My husband, Bill, and I have worked as hospice volunteers, watching the transitions of beautiful human beings—transitions that took our patients from this earth to that next plane where they continue to live in a totally soul-state. And each life was perfect.

I sat with a dear friend who left us so peacefully that I said to her son, "Watching your mother die taught me how to live." Her life was not always easy but, again, it was perfect.

All of our lives come together over the years like the piecing of a quilt, patch by colorful patch. What I have experienced in this lifetime has made me who I am today, just as what you have experienced has made you who you are. With each trial and joy we learn to walk our life paths one minute at a time. We learn to just sit and "be" when we are ill because those are the metaphorical moments that teach us how to stay quiet and listen to the Great Mystery. And then we run outside and "play" when we are at the height of our wellness, dancing and singing with the Beloved.

It's up to us to make our lives perfect—changing those things that need changing and accepting those things that cannot be changed. Giving thanks for EVERYTHING!

Affirmation: I live one minute at a time, reveling in each and every experience.

NAMASTE

January 3
A New Beginning

"The examined life is not worth living."
-Socrates

Here we are into the third day of a new year and, once again, I am sitting on my front porch contemplating this new beginning and reminiscing over the year just past.

Instead of dwelling on the mistakes I have made, I have chosen to forgive myself and move on to open a new chapter in my life.

In some ways, the year ahead will resemble the one just passed. I will continue to read and write, to attend my Spiritual Center and its many functions and to enjoy each holiday and the many parties with my family and friends.

In other instances, my days will differ as I make a conscious choice to listen more carefully to the Beloved, realizing, as never before, that I am a spiritual being having the allness of Infinite Love, Infinite Mind.

I will change my "thinking" to "knowing" that, because of divine law, all things are possible. I will give up the idea of "fate" or "luck" and believe as Emerson did when he said, "The dice of God are always loaded."

Affirmation: Today, I don't "think" I can succeed, I "know" I can succeed.

NAMASTE

January 4

Find Your Sanctuary

"The world was all before them, where to choose their place of rest. . ."
-John Milton

A quiet peacefulness washes over me this morning while I sit in my sanctuary, in my tweed, cup-like chair. Across from where I perch, a shabby-chic armoire rests on the carpeted floor. On top of this armoire reside the pictures of my "grandies" and "great-grandies." In my thinking, their smiling faces spring to life, and I hear the words, "I love you."

In this same room, there is a bookcase housing the multiple volumes that hold my interest—spark my mind—feed my soul. A picture of a meditative woman graces a small table next to my chair. Also, on this table, is a diary and a pencil holder with more pencils than I can ever use (all sharpened to a fine point—one of my idiosyncrasies). This sanctuary is a "my place" kind of room that contains within its walls my aura—my essence.

We all need such a place—a sanctuary where we can retreat from the world, charge our spiritual batteries and connect with God. If you don't have a spare room in your home, just a chair with a small table sitting beside it will do. On that table you can keep your favorite books, magazines and, perhaps, a journal.

Stroll through your home today and let your intuition lead you to that perfect nook to house your "sacred sanctuary."

Affirmation: I have a perfect sanctuary.

NAMASTE

January 5
A Soul Experience

"I have liberated my soul."
Saint Bernard, Epistle 371

How do you envision yourself? Are you a body housing a soul or are you a soul walking about the earth as flesh and blood? Someone who God created so that He could experience life through your eyes and ears?

I like to think I am the latter. It makes me want to "show Spirit a good time"—to allow Him a co-creating experience with me and I with Him. I want to breathe in the essence of the Beloved each day, to walk hand-in-Divine-hand as I write, shop, cook, clean or sit on my front porch watching a red-throated hummingbird perch on the bottle-shaped feeder and suckle sweet sugar-water.

How would our lives be gladdened if we only realized that the Divine is constantly with us, dancing and skipping alongside us through the darks and the lights of our mortal experience? Holding us close when we need that Mother-Father love and sitting beside us, guiding our fingers when we write our novels or our poetry or when we splash paint to canvass, or as our yarn becomes afghans and our materials become colorful quilts. It's called co-creation and it's the only way to live in this world—truly live!

God isn't "up there," He's an inside job—a living, breathing part of us. Never further away than the beating of our hearts or the blood that rushes through our veins.

Feel Her. Listen to Him.

Affirmation: I am a soul experiencing life as a human being.

NAMASTE

January 6
Ten Slow Breaths

"Breathing deeply and slowly, I descend into the emptiness of peace."
-Author

There is a breathing technique that is both curative and relaxing. It involves taking ten slow, deep breaths and the imaging of a stairway. You can do it anywhere and at any time.

Close your eyes and imagine yourself standing at the top of a flight of ten stairs. Slowly, counting backwards from ten to one, see yourself descending down, one step at a time.

Inhale fully through your nose and then exhale slowly through your mouth as you say the number and take a downward step.

You will find that, with each tread, you come closer and closer to relaxation.

When you reach the bottom of the staircase, your tension will have lessened and you will feel calm.

Affirmation: I mentally take ten steps down a stairway, achieving complete relaxation.

NAMASTE

January 7

God Hears And Answers Our Every Prayer

"But truly God has listened; He has given heed to the words of my prayer."
-Psalm 66:19

There is a lovely woman who attends the Spiritual Center where I worship each Sunday. Nancy has been appointed "Prayer Partner" for the Center and when we or one of our loved ones have a special need, we give that request to her. Nancy holds that person in prayer each day for two weeks, or longer if we ask. There is a radiance to this woman—a radiance that exudes a beautiful, angelic aura. And I'm sure that sacred immanency mirrors her life—a life spent in prayer and meditation and in counseling others.

At one of our recent "Women's Wisdom" meetings, Nancy ended her presentation with a very moving prayer. I asked her if she would write it down so that I could include it in this book and she graciously did so.

I present the prayer to you, my readers, in the hope that it will touch you as deeply as it did me.

"I pray that all of your most cherished dreams and visions come true. I pray that your heart's desires are fulfilled in miraculous and wonderful ways. I pray your life is free of fear and pain, and that all you do is a blessing to everyone you meet. I know Spirit is with you, and that you are continually aware of the Divine Presence.

"Even more, I pray as you use this awesome power of prayer that you come to know your Spiritual Source so intimately that you experience the deep joy of knowing, . . . that the God who created you, talks and listens to you, guides and walks with you, will never, ever desert you . . . for we are one with Spirit.

"And for that I say, thank you, thank you, Mother, Father, God.

"And so it is.

"Amen."

Affirmation: My prayers reach out, blessing my loved ones and the world.

NAMASTE

January 8

The Older I Get, the "Funner" Life Gets

"I actively participate in regressive aging."
-Liz Sigel

When you get to my age things change—for the better, I might add. What my children used to think of as "mom being silly" now comes off as, "Look, isn't she cute?" What they don't know is that I'm just as silly in this present behavior as I was thirty or forty years ago. (The white hair and wrinkles fool 'em every time!)

We need to maintain our sense of fun as we age, even rev it up a few RPMs.

Try dancing through the house with "oldies but goodies" blasting from your boom boxes or iPods (just be sure there aren't any area rugs to stumble over.)

Go to your senior pool and get a little crazy with the other "girls" in exercise group. Or maybe take a Tai Chi class and out float the instructor.

You might try belly dancing. At our age we have more belly to work with—twice the fun! (Don't get jealous, you younger gals! Someday you'll have more tummy to work with, too.)

No matter what age you are or what you choose to do for enjoyment put your whole heart into it! Remember that God is in every part of our lives. It's all spiritual—even, and most especially, our times of fun.

Affirmation: Today I will dance and sing with life.

NAMASTE

What Are Your Dreams?

> "Go confidently in the direction of your dreams.
> Live the life you've imagined."
> -Henry David Thoreau

What are your dreams? What do you imagine for yourself? What do you hunger for?

I woke up one morning with a complete plot for a novel dancing through my head. I got up, wrote the outline on a piece of paper and started, that day, to write *Margo*, a book, that, with the help of a dynamic critique group is now published.

So, please, don't put off your dreams. Take a quilting class, that painting course, or those piano or flute lessons. Maybe even get that college degree you've always wanted.

Remember, we all came to this earth to answer a special call, to use those wonderful gifts that God bestowed upon us.

Embrace that for which you were born.

Affirmation: Today I will go confidently in the direction of my dreams.

NAMASTE

January 10
The Freeway of Our Lives

"God is the center line on the freeway of our lives."
-Author

Inside my sanctuary, it is very quiet this morning. Outside the traffic on the freeway flows in a steady, humming stream. My thoughts and prayers go out to those who are, today, traveling to their various destinations.

Life is like that freeway—going to and coming from. Each day, my morning quiet time with God brings me a different experience. Sometimes, I go to that place where I allow myself to be so filled with the Beloved that my heart nearly bursts. Other times, I come from a darker side, a place of pain or loss and I simply allow myself to be embraced by the comforting arms of Infinite Love.

The freeways of our lives bring us both light and heavy traffic. But always—always, God is the center line, guiding us to our destinations, guiding us home.

Affirmation: I travel the freeway of life with God as my center line.

NAMASTE

The Echo of Life

"Our life is a mirror of our own doings."
-Author unknown

I recently heard this story and would like to share it with you. It is written by one of my favorite authors, Unknown.

"A man and his son were walking in the forest. Suddenly the boy trips and feeling a sharp pain, he screams, 'Ahhhhhh!' Surprised, he hears a voice coming from the mountain, 'Ahhhhhh!'

Filled with curiosity, the boy screams, 'Who are you?' But the only answer he receives is 'Who are you?' This makes him angry, so he screams, 'You are a coward!'

And the voice answers, 'You are a coward!'

He looks at his father, asking, 'Dad, what is going on?'

Son,' the man replies, 'pay attention.' Then he screams, 'I admire you!' The voice answers, 'I admire you!" The father shouts, 'You are wonderful!' and the voice answers, 'You are wonderful!'

Then the father explains, 'People call this ECHO, but truly it is LIFE!

Life always gives you back what you give out. Life is a mirror of your actions. If you want more love, give more love. If you want understanding, give understanding.

If you want people to be patient and respectful to you, give patience and respect. This rule of nature applies to every aspect of our lives.

Life always gives you back what you give out. Your life is not a coincidence; it is a mirror of your own doings."

Affirmation: I live my life so that it echoes back positive, loving words and experiences.

NAMASTE

January 12
An Attitude of Gratitude

"Gratitude is not only the greatest of virtues, but the parent of all the others."
-Marcus Tullius Cicero

This morning I'm thinking about what I am grateful for, and there is so much!

All of us have things for which we are grateful. Some of them will be the same—our homes, families, friends, our furry pets, our gardens that bring us delightful colors and aromas. But some will be personally our own—our cancer, the loss of a loved one, or various other "dark nights of the soul."

Yes, there is always something for which to be grateful, even during difficult times.

I have had periods in my life when I didn't think I could possibly endure another day of pain. During one of those times, I came upon a quote from Saint John of the Cross. He wrote, "The dark night is simply part of the mystical journey to our oneness with God."

After reading those words, I began to see the dark nights of my soul as essential—my spiritual growth could not be attained without them. During these challenges, I spent more time with the Beloved. In honoring my dark nights of the soul, I learned to trust and know that I am never alone. And neither are you, dear friend.

Affirmation: Being God's love in expression, my every experience brings me closer to the Infinite One.

NAMASTE

January 13

The Piano Lesson

"Anything can be accomplished with the guidance
of The Master's hand."
-Author

Today, I have another story to tell, one that was written anonymously and, oh, so beautifully!

"Wishing to encourage her young son's progress on the piano, a mother took the small boy to a Paderewski concert. After they were seated, the mother spotted a friend in the audience and walked down the aisle to greet her.

Seizing the opportunity to explore the wonders of the concert hall, the little boy rose and eventually explored his way through a door marked "NO ADMITTANCE." When the house lights dimmed and the concert was about to begin, the mother returned to her seat and discovered that her son was missing.

Suddenly, the curtains parted and spotlights focused on the impressive Steinway on stage. In horror, the mother saw her little boy sitting at the keyboard, innocently picking out "Twinkle, Twinkle Little Star."

At that moment, the great piano master made his entrance, quickly moved to the piano, and whispered in the boy's ear, "Don't quit." "Keep playing."

Then leaning over, Paderewski reached down with his left hand and began filling in a bass part. Soon his right arm reached around to the other side of the child and he added a running obbligato.

Together, the old master and the young novice transformed a frightening situation into a wonderfully creative experience. The audience was mesmerized.

That's the way it is with God. What we can accomplish on our own is hardly noteworthy. We try our best, but the results aren't exactly graceful flowing music. But with the hand of the Master, our life's work truly can be beautiful.

Next time you set out to accomplish great feats, listen carefully. You can hear the voice of the Master, whispering in your ear, "Don't quit." Keep playing." Feel His loving arms around you. Know that His strong hands are playing the concerto of your life.

Remember, God doesn't call the equipped. He equips the called. And he'll always be there to love and guide you on to great things."

Affirmation: I listen to the Master and hear him whisper "keep playing."

NAMASTE

Life is to be Lived

"Life is meant to be lived. If you sit it out because you might make a
mistake you're not playing the game of life."
-Gail Maishor. RScP
From Here to Serenity

My Great Aunt Mae was a regular Mary Poppins with an attitude—
an over-the-top attitude of playfulness and glee. In her late sixties and
seventies, it was part of her summer fun to don a well-used black
bathing suit and join us kids in the front yard to jump in and out of an
old galvanized tub and have water fights with the hose. She loved with
fervor and played the same way. Aunt Mae lived with my grandparents
in Sacramento, California and was the one who normally fed and
nurtured the family dog, Chico. That brown-and-white collie loved
Aunt Mae as much as we did—maybe more.

I would like to share with you an article from the Sacramento Bee
Newspaper. I have only a copy and not the original, but it was written
sometime in the mid-40s. It was Aunt Mae's obituary:

DOG WILL PAY FINAL TRIBUTE TO MISTRESS

"More than nine months ago County Hospital officials were upset
and puzzled when they learned that a pure-bred, brown-and-white
collie had eluded the rule against dogs in the institution and bounded
onto the bed of an aged patient.

They started to protest that Chico, an attractive dog though he was,
couldn't be allowed to violate the regulations. They learned how Chico
had disappeared from his home at 3238 Donner Way and had taken
several days to find his friend, Mrs. Mae Oppenheim.

At 75, Mrs. Oppenheim had been taken to the hospital early in
January and for several weeks Chico wandered disconsolately around
the house, particularly about 4 P.M. each day when he usually had
been fed by "Aunt Mae." His disappearance was solved when Mrs.

Oppenheim heard a low whine outside her hospital window the night of January 14. She pretty much discounted the idea that it was Chico until a very muddy and sand-covered collie bounced onto her bed and showered her with the only kind of affection a loving dog can show.

Mr. and Mrs. Frank S. Pritchard, with whom Mrs. Oppenheim lived, explained about the close relationship between the aged woman and the collie. Virtually every night after that, Chico had accompanied the Pritchards on their nightly visits to Mrs. Oppenheim. Each night, the dog greeted his beloved friend, then retired to an out-of-the-way spot under her bed.

Today Chico won't be out of the way for one second. In fact, he will have a special place of honor when funeral services are conducted for Mrs. Oppenheim."

So, you see, it wasn't just my Aunt Mae who refused to sit life out, it was Chico as well.

Affirmation: I know that life is meant to be lived, mistakes and all.

NAMASTE

What Makes You Happy?

"Most people are about as happy as they make their minds up to be."
-Abraham Lincoln

What makes you happy? For me, it's writing, wrapping up in a warm quilt, going to a party—I love a good party! And then there's meditating or eating a "yummy" piece of chocolate.

When we experience happiness, our body's natural opiates, or endorphins, are released, making us feel better—more alive!

Write down five things that make you happy. Maybe they are things that you haven't done for a long time and that you should start doing again.

Even during our crisis times we can remain in a state of happiness. Just listen to the words of this ancient Chinese proverb, "There is chaos under the heavens and the situation is excellent."

Affirmation: I make up my mind, daily, to be happy.

NAMASTE

Living a Soul-Centered Life

"Waste no more time talking about great souls and how they should be.
Become one yourself!"
-Marcus Aurelius

Someone once told me that when Mother Teresa was asked what she thought her life's mission was, she was purported to have answered, "I am a pencil in the hand of God who is writing a love letter to the world."

What a beautiful statement that was—as beautiful as the gentle woman herself.

I pondered that question, not only for myself, but for everyone else as well. This is what came to me: "We are all children of the Beloved, living a soul-centered life."

Just what does it mean to be "soul-centered?"

Within each of us is a "piece of God." This piece of God is our soul. It is that part of us that, like Spirit, is infinite—immortal. It is our "God-ness."

We have a choice to either recognize our "God-ness" or to ignore it. To ignore it usually creates havoc in our psyches as well as our lives. To recognize it and use its powers is what I call "living a soul-centered life."

Affirmation: I lovingly choose to recognize my "God-ness."

NAMASTE

What Will You Do for the Rest of Your Life?

"What we have called our "middle age" need not be a
turning point toward death."
-Marianne Williamson
The Age of Miracles
Embracing the new midlife

In her book, *The Age of Miracles*, Marianne Williamson asks the question, "What will I do with the time I still have left?"

What a provocative query!

It caused me to pause and think about my own life. So far, I've slurped up every moment like a parched puppy does water.

But what now?

This second, this minute, this hour is all I have. I long to breathe in every experience, every emotion and let them fill me as though drinking from a very large tumbler of "joy juice."

I want every day to ring like the Bells of Saint Mary's—to walk through the rest of my life experiencing Vivaldi's Four Seasons—a symphony of spring, summer, fall and winter—to dance the ballet of contentment and sing the arias of a life well-lived and well-loved.

I wish to stroll hand-in-hand with the Beloved along the sands of time and, at life's end, slip through that thin veil to the other side where I will continue the eternal pleasures of life.

Affirmation: I will someday step into eternity, knowing I have lived a full, life.

NAMASTE

January 18
Following God's Divine Plan

"Men are born to succeed, not fail."
-Henry David Thoreau

How many times have we hesitated to follow our bliss because we thought we might fail, our family might not approve or "the moon was not yet in the seventh house?"

You get what I mean, I'm sure. Mom wanted you to be a doctor, dad wanted you to be a lawyer and Aunt Midge insisted that the family needed an in-house psychiatrist.

So, now, while you're sitting in your Freudian-decorated office listening to Patient Number Four share his woes, (Aunt Midge won) you find yourself sketching a house that could very well be featured in the next issue of Architectural Digest.

What we love to do is exactly what we were created to do. It comes straight from Divine Wisdom. The importance of listening to that still small voice within cannot be over-emphasized. We need to teach that to our children—let them choose their careers with the help of that voice, not the voice of Aunt Midge.

Listen carefully and let Divine Intelligence answer these two questions: "What is my heart's desire and how can I change things in order to follow that desire?"

Affirmation: I was born to succeed.

NAMASTE

January 19
Manifesting Love

"That best portion of a good man's life, his little, nameless,
unremembered acts of kindness and love."
-William Wordsworth

I don't think we can emphasize enough what love can do for each of us as well as for the collective universe.

Look around you everyday to discover how you can express the love that is the biggest part of who you really are—tell that perfect stranger how beautiful she is, hug that rebellious kid, sit for a moment next to that elderly lady alone and sad in the park, letting her know that God truly does love her.

Allow that erupting love to rise from the depths of your soul like lava from an active volcano, overflowing into goodness and grace. And then let the rock that hardens from the cooling lava become the solid foundation on which you build your golden castle to house the benevolent affection of God.

In his book, Spiritual Liberation, Michael Bernard Beckwith writes, "As you mature spiritually, you ask life a different set of questions. Instead of 'Where can I find love?' you ask, 'How can I radiate love?' You transcend wanting to be loved. It's natural to want to be loved, but when you mature, this desire doesn't develop into a needy personality. It shifts from desperately asking, 'Isn't anybody going to love me?' to "How can I express more love in my life.' Then, from the center of your Self there will radiate a divine love so potent that you will begin to fall in love with being loving . . . ."

Affirmation: Today I fall in love with being loving!

NAMASTE

January 20
We Are All Part of The Boston Pops

"Is not music the food of love?"
-Richard Sheridan

Clouds scurry across the sky this morning almost in rhythm to the music of the Boston Pops Orchestra that wafts from my house and onto the front porch.

When I think of my life in musical terms, I pick out each instrument and compare its similarity to my dance with the Beloved.

The drums of my heart rhythmically beat out a tempo of love and compassion for my family, friends, and all of humanity.

The trill of the flutes carries through the air notes of gratitude—gratitude for all that life has given me: the good and the bad, the abundance and the lack, the dark and the light.

The strings of the violin sing out the joy of being alive, for having been given a physical body in which to relish this earthly walk, making it a magical stroll with the Great Creator.

The brass section trumpets the Universal strength, resilience and power within me, allowing the confidence needed to live a full and productive life.

In our oneness with God, we become an orchestra of faith—a symphony of harmonic love.

Affirmation: I am a part of God's universal orchestra.

NAMASTE

January 21
Oh, Death Where is Thy Sting?

"Even death cannot take from us the closeness of our relationships, for it is in the bonding of love that our togetherness prevails."
-Author

Death is merely the final stage of life. In dying, we disappear behind the veil to the "other side," and our soul becomes free of all things physical, going back to its natural, blessed state. I personally prefer to think of "death" as people "making their transition."

There is no doubt that when someone we love makes that transition, there is a giant void in our lives. Grief, like a great tsunami, washes over us, leaving us emotionally wounded and physically drained.

When my former husband died, I spent many sleepless nights crying out, "Why? Why?" He was fifty-seven years old, far too young, or so I thought. And I was a forty-nine-year-old widow wondering how I could possibly go on living without that funny, loving man.

I slowly emerged from my mourning, realizing that I was strong in places I didn't even know. I was still a part of life and had a responsibility to myself to live it fully, knowing that I still had more to accomplish.

I eventually shed the heavy cloak of sadness, replacing it with the lighter, silken scarf of joy—the joy of having known and having loved this wonderful man.

Affirmation: I allow myself to grieve a loved one with the knowledge that even death cannot take from me the closeness of our relationship.

NAMASTE

January 22

The Woman Inside of You

"There is in every woman's heart a spark of heavenly fire . . ."
-Washington Irving

An unknown author has written a piece entitled *The Woman Next to You*. I have taken the liberty to rename it The Woman Inside of You, and to change some of the words.

The woman inside of you is the greatest miracle and the greatest mystery at this moment, a testament of God living in our midst.

The woman inside of you is a unique universe of experience, seething with necessity and possibility, dread and desire, smiles and frowns, laughter and tears, fears and hopes, all struggling for expression.

The woman inside of you is surging to become something in particular, to arrive at some destination, to have a story and a song, to be known, to know.

The woman inside of you believes in something—something precious. She stands for something, labors for something, waits for something, runs for something, runs towards something.

The woman inside of you has problems and fears and wonders how she is doing, but she is endowed with a great toughness in the face of adversity, able to survive the most unbelievable difficulties and persecutions.

The woman inside of you can do something better than anyone else in the world.

The woman inside of you can live not only for herself, but also for others.

The woman inside of you is more than any description or explanation. That woman can never be fully controlled nor should be.

Now that you know that woman inside of you, ask yourself these questions:

1. Who have been your female role models or influences? What about them do you admire?
2. Have you ever found yourself feeling stuck, stagnant, lost or confused - especially in relation to your sense of yourself as a spiritual being and a woman?
3. What is something you have not yet accomplished in your life, but would like to?

Your answers may surprise you and they might give you more understanding as to who that woman inside of you really is.

Affirmation: I love and respect that woman within me.

NAMASTE

January 23
Are You A Perfectionist?

"No perfection is so absolute that some impurity doth not pollute."
-William Shakespeare

While rummaging through my bathroom armoire the other day, I found a pillowslip enhanced with a bit of artistic crochet at its opening. It was also faultlessly embroidered with tiny, delicate white roses along the width of its hem.

The slip was wrapped in yellowing tissue paper. After taking it from its wrapping, and upon careful inspection, I discovered a small tear separating the lacy crochet from the linen pillowcase.

Being a consummate perfectionist, I ran to get my box of threads, all color-coordinated, of course. But while removing a large spool of white thread, I could almost hear the pillowslip begging to be left as it was—to be like the tattered, stuffed bunny in Margery Williams' book, *The Velveteen Rabbit*—well-loved in its imperfections.

So, carelessly throwing the spool of thread back into the box, I closed the lid and then threw the tissue paper in the trash.

I imagined a gentle sigh emanating from the torn pillowcase as I replaced it in the armoire snuggled up against a set of well-worn, rose-printed sheets.

Being a perfectionist is both a blessing and a curse. It carries with it the joy of a well-organized home and the burden of constant picking up and cleaning and sometimes the bickering between a husband and wife—one being "Mrs. Perfect," and the other "Mr. Not-So-Much."

I think it's time to let go of my "perfectionism," to maybe leave a bit of clutter here-and-there. It would certainly free my life to answer the calling of my soul—to listen to God in longer meditations and write to my heart's content while the dishes and the dust pile up.

Maybe I'll try it for just a couple of days. Who knows, I might even enjoy it!

Affirmation: I let go of perfectionism to answer the calling of my soul.

NAMASTE

January 24

Expanding our Horizons

"When our inner vision opens, our horizons expand."
-Louise L. Hay
The Power is Within You

From my front porch this morning, I watch as threads of clouds lace the sky and then, one-by-one, disappear into the atmosphere, leaving patches of pure blue, a metaphor of what Louise Hay said in the opening quote—When the clouds, "our inner vision, opens," the blue sky, "our horizons, expand."

We need only two things to accomplish the opening of our vision and the expanding of our horizons—the Infinite, All Wise Creator and ourselves. Our faith in that Law of Creation is what triggers the grinding of the wheels of our finite minds, allowing the manufacturing of ideas that eventually turn into best-selling books, award-winning art work, astounding inventions, haute couture and architectural wonders.

All we need do is picture in our minds what we want, feel the inimitable joy and passion of having it and work diligently toward the final outcome.

Affirmation: My faith in God allows me to co-create with Him.

NAMASTE

Instruments of Peace

"First keep the peace within yourself, then you can
also bring peace to others."
-Thomas á Kempis

A most beautiful prayer is the prayer of Saint Francis of Assisi. Today, I would like to share it with you.

Lord, make me an instrument of thy peace.
Where there is hatred, let me sow love;
Where there is injury, pardon;
Where there is despair, hope;
Where there is darkness, light;
Where there is sadness, joy.

O divine Master, grant that I may not so much seek
To be consoled as to console,
To be understood as to understand,
To be loved as to love;
For it is in giving that we receive;
It is in pardoning that we are pardoned;
It is in dying to self that we are born to eternal life.
-Attributed to Saint Francis of Assisi

Affirmation: I am an instrument of peace.

NAMASTE

Personal Identity

"We are all perfectly formed masterpieces, created by the Infinite One."
-Author

It delights me so when I look closely at my finger tips. Those tiny, ridged lines are but another bit of proof that I am a wonderful, one-of-a-kind human being.

God gave each of us our own personal identity; the tips of our fingers are an absolute confirmation that we are each separate creations.

Out of the millions of people in the world, there are no two who have fingerprints alike! How awesome is that?

Only the great mind of God could take the rounded ridges of the skin on our fingers and individualize them millions of times over.

We are all magically and perfectly formed masterpieces of the Infinite One.

Affirmation: I thank God for my individuality.

NAMASTE

Prayer

"More things are wrought by prayer than this world dreams of."
-Tennyson

Prayer is the universal language of the soul. Recently I took a six-week course entitled "Pathways to Prayer." The class was written and facilitated by my dear friend, Nancy Nisonger. Nancy uses a unique and very effective method to talk to the Beloved. She entitled it "The Call," and explained that it is just another route down the pathway to prayer.

With her permission, I would like to present "The Call" to you.

INTENTION – Before you begin to pray, go into the silence and ask for clarity. When your mind is clear, state your intention. (I am going to use my own prayer concerning this book, since I had just started writing it at the time I took the class.) "My intention is to co-create with Spirit as I write *Welcome To My Front Porch*."

CONNECTING with your Higher Power – Just like dialing up, or calling on someone in person, you are now ready to begin your conversation. Your prayer might start by expressing your relationship with your Higher Power. I began this way: "Dear Beloved Spirit, our journey together through all of these years has been one of both 'dark nights of the soul' and many incredible moments of joy. Through it all, You have carried me, like a child, in Your loving, protecting arms."

ACCEPTING THE TRUTH – This is where you make your acceptance of a "truth statement." Everything is in the now; that is why we don't use words such as "maybe," "someday," or "I wish." For this, I said, "As I write my book, I know that you will guide my thoughts and ideas, for you, God, are the Author within me."

LETTING IT GO – Now you turn everything over to the Supreme Source. You might say, "I release and let go so that you, God, can do your work. I know with certainty that my book is already written in the Universe and will soon be published here on earth."

LIVING AND LOVING – You have come full circle in your prayer. You are a beloved child of God, and you were sent here to fulfill a purpose. You could end with expressions of gratitude or awareness. For this, I said, "I give thanks for my gift of writing and my gift of loving others, and, most of all, I am thankful for You, my omnipotent co-creator. And so it is. Amen."

I came home from class the day Nancy presented this positive, effective way of praying and not only wrote the above prayer, but also several others. I prayed that the baby shower I was hosting the following Sunday would go smoothly, I prayed for my health, for my children and my husband, and for peace.

Try this method of prayer and see how it works for you. It is such a peaceful way to talk to the Infinite Giver.

Affirmation: Today, I will manifest my desires through prayer.

NAMASTE

January 28
We Are All Jewels Tucked in a Common Net

"Everything and everyone is interconnected and interdependent."
-Author

Or as John Donne said, "No man is an island."

In our interconnectedness, we all depend on each other. What one of us does affects all of us.

Buddhist concepts hold that everything is closely connected. This idea is communicated in the net of the Vedic god, Indra, whose net hangs over his palace. This Indra's net has a multifaceted jewel at each vertex, and each jewel is reflected in every one of the other jewels so that there is a brilliant mirroring activity going on at all times.

I love this concept! I love thinking about each one of us as a sparkling jewel placed in the universe to reflect all of the other dazzling jewels, so that the process of divine mirroring is infinite

Affirmation: I am a jewel in the universal net of humanity.

NAMASTE

Love is the Common Denominator

"Love is all we have, the only way that each can help the other."
-Euripides

It is wonderful to see the common ground in each of the world's great traditions. The Golden Rule is captured in so many of these faiths:

"Hurt not others in ways that you yourself would find hurtful."
BUDDHA

"What is hateful to you, do not to your fellow man." JUDAISM

"Do unto others as you would have them do unto you." CHRISTIANITY

"Blessed is he who blesses his brother." BAHA'I

"No one of you is a believer until he desires for his brother that which he desires for himself." ISLAM

"Do not wrong or hate your neighbor. For it is not he who you wrong but yourself." NATIVE AMERICAN SPIRITUALITY

"Don't create enmity with anyone as God is within everyone."
SIKHISM

"Regard your neighbor's gain as your own gain, and your neighbor's loss as your own loss." TAOISM

"Be charitable to all beings, love is the representative of God."
SHINTO

Affirmation: I can see that all faiths embrace that beautiful principle of love.

NAMASTE

January 30

Just Hit the "Delete" Key

"Most of us carry some degree of guilt for something we may or may
not have done. Dear One, please know that God does not hold
anything we have done against us. We are loved more deeply than we
can know. We are a part of God, and God cannot hate Itself."
-Gail Manishor, RScP
From Here to Serenity

I love the delete key on my computer. It erases all of my mistakes and
misspellings and lets me start over.

I use my inner delete key to do the same thing.

My deletion process is easy. I merely ask forgiveness from those I
have hurt and then forgive myself for actions or words that I regard as
wrong, or thoughtless, or cruel.

Then I try not to repeat them again.

God forgives us and views us only as perfect souls, so why don't we
do the same for ourselves?

By releasing our past, and sometimes present "goofs," no matter
how big or small, we can then be free to go on and live the life for
which we were intended.

Affirmation: I forgive myself with love and understanding.

NAMASTE

January 31

The Zen of Nesting

"Ah! There is nothing like staying at home for real comfort."
-Jane Austin

There was a time when I disagreed with Jane Austin. I loved my home, but I wasn't always comfortable within its four walls.

During a forced two-year confinement due to illness, I mostly lay in bed, reading. Along with the books that deepened my spiritual faith, I also studied the art of Feng Shui.

Through the help of catalogs and my ever-so-patient husband, who would run out and purchase whatever small piece of furniture or table décor I happened to see advertised in the morning paper, we redecorated our living room.

Satisfied with the "Zen" feeling that permeated the refurbished front room, we moved our redecorating frenzy into our very ample kitchen. In a matter of a month or so, Bill painted all of our cabinets white with red trim and then went antiquing to purchase accessories that turned our kitchen into a red-and-white retro 40s heaven.

Now, I can say with Jane, "There is nothing like staying at home for real comfort."

Sit quietly in your living room for a short time and breath in its essence—feel its spiritual energy, or lack thereof. Then close your eyes and picture it in a way that would make you feel more comfortable—more peaceful.

It doesn't have to cost a fortune to make it your "heaven-on-earth;" with just a picture here or a special candle there or maybe a small interesting table purchased from your local thrift shop you can have a whole new world.

Affirmation: Today I fill my home with my own spirit of authenticity.

NAMASTE

Loving Ourselves and Others

"Thou shalt love the Lord thy God with all thy heart, and with all thy
soul . . . and thy neighbor as thyself."
-Luke 10:27

Isn't it wonderful how God shows us in the above verse that we definitely
need to love ourselves first when he says, "and thy neighbor as thyself."

In order to receive love, we must first love ourselves. It is then that
we understand our own worth and can freely accept the love of others.
We all love because that is who we truly are. It is our natural state—our
nature.

Each one of us is an expression of Infinite Love, and, as such, we all
need to give and receive that most cherished of feelings.

As a connected chain of humanity, the need for giving and receiving
love is so powerful that a missing link—one who is incapable of giving
or receiving love—can break the golden chain.

Once we learn to appreciate and love ourselves, we can then pass
that unconditional love to others and the chain remains complete.

Affirmation: I love myself and others unconditionally.

NAMASTE

February 2
Grace

"Love is the beauty of the soul."
-St. Augustine

In the dictionary, the theological meaning of grace is defined as:
    a. The freely, unmerited favor and love of God.
    b. The influence or spirit of God operating in humans to
       regenerate or strengthen them.
    c. A virtue or excellence of divine origin.
    For me, it's:
    d. All of the above.

Today, God's grace seems to be graciously supplying me with inspiring thoughts on grace. (Redundancy definitely intended!)

To me, grace is simply the outpouring of God's love, that constant flow of good in my life. It has also been defined as God's unconditional love and acceptance. I adore that definition! We cannot even begin to comprehend God's awesome grace, a love so perfect that there are simply no human words to describe it.

There is nothing I can do to earn or be deprived of the unequivocal love of my Creator who sees me as a kind and loving creation, deserving of everything good.

When we align ourselves with the truth of God's grace, we can then view others as loving creations, as soul-connected brothers and sisters.

The gift of grace is bestowed upon each and every one of us, simply because we are all children of God.

Affirmation: By God's grace, I am blessed beyond words.

NAMASTE

February 3
Making Love to the World

"Work each day in your creative garden."
-Author

I love to work each day in my creative garden, sowing it with the seeds of my God-given gift. Then I can watch as each small bud blossoms into a spectacular bloom of that which I hunger after, my authentic achievements.

Start your garden today by doing what you enjoy more than anything else in the world—the thing that makes you forget what time it is, that consumes you to the point of ecstatic distraction.

In time, you will harvest the crop of your passion simply by doing that which you love.

Affirmation: Today I plant a creative garden and discover my way of making love to the world.

NAMASTE

February 4
Living in the Now

"Don't miss the joys of today by dwelling on the less than joyful
memories of yesterday."
-Author

Part of "living in the now" includes recognition, forgiveness and release.
We can't deny an unhappy childhood, a broken relationship or the
loss of a loved one, but neither do we need to dwell on these past
experiences. We can recognize the hurt, forgive the one who hurt us
and release the emotions. An affirmation that I found in Louise L. Hay's
book, *You Can Heal Your Life*, has helped me enormously. Each day, I
affirm, "I joyously release the past. I am at peace."

It is definitely important to mourn each hurtful encounter, but, it is
even more important, to recognize that these experiences are simply
the Beloved shaping us into who we are, then moving us onto another
path—a new adventure.

If we can stay in "the now" instead of slipping back to "what was"
or thinking of "what might be," we will find ourselves living joyously
with the Infinite Presence.

Affirmation: Today, I will live constantly in "the now," releasing "the
past" and letting go of "what might be," living a joyous, spontaneous
life.

NAMASTE

Let's Have a Party!

"The guests are met, the feast is set: May'st hear the merry din."
-Samuel Taylor Coleridge

Recently my husband and I hosted a baby shower for a young couple from our Spiritual Center. It was a gala affair with thirty-two people in attendance—a couple's party. For some of the men, it was their first experience at a baby shower, and many of them said they loved it—even the "silly" games.

Our living room and dining room were decorated with indoor trees resplendent with hundreds of twinkling lights and decorated in a "baby girl" theme. My adored front porch sparkled with a dozen lit candles. It was a glorious party filled with love and laughter.

When we invite people into our homes, we also invite them to see us as we really are. Our choice of decorating always portrays our individuality. The furnishings, the colors, the pictures and the knick-knacks depict our personalities. Our homes sing a beautiful anthem of everyday living—everyday loving.

When the shower was over and everyone had gone, I dimmed the lights and sat in solitude, reliving the party, knowing that each one who had attended had left behind their beautiful imprint, their aura, in order that I might feel a trace of their loving presence forever in my home and in my heart.

Having a social gathering, no matter the number of attendees, will bring you great joy and you will find the walls around you echoing with good times and love long after the guests have departed.

Affirmation: Today I will bring joy into my home and into my life.

NAMASTE

February 6
The Divine Flow of God

"I am an expression of the Divine Flow of God."
-Author

There is a creek outside my living room window that flows into a small pond. Today, as a result of a five day rain storm, the great quantity of water pouring into the creek has caused it to move along more rapidly.

The stream reminds me of the Divine Flow of God. When we allow the blessings of the Beloved to rain upon us, through our love, our giving and our openness to His leading, we are like that creek, full and rushing to our destination—that calling to which we were born.

Affirmation: I stay centered in God and flow swiftly into the pond of my calling.

NAMASTE

February 7
How Do We Learn?

"We learn well and fast when we experience the consequences of
what we do—and don't do."
-Anonymous

Like the threads in a tapestry, there are so many teachers who weave in
and out of our lives. Our parents, educators, and spiritual teachers all
indoctrinate us with lessons that mold and shape us as human beings.

My most significant teachers have been life's experiences. The
things that I have accomplished as well as the mistakes that I have
made, have taught me that I can choose how to live, and sometimes
re-choose.

Nature itself is a natural professor. Watching the rain fall allows me
the tactile sense of renewal. Birds teach me to live in the moment, not
worrying about yesterday or tomorrow—just accepting what God is
offering me right now. A delicate lily opens its petals and, in turn, my
heart opens to the joys and blessing of everyday life.

Henry David Thoreau expressed learning so beautifully when he
wrote, "I went to the woods because I wished to live deliberately, to
front only the essential facts of life, and see if I could not learn what it
had to teach, and not, when I came to die, discover that I had not lived."

Affirmation: I thank God for all of the wonderful teachers in my life.

NAMASTE

February 8

Joy

"Joy is my compass It leads me everywhere I need to go."
Michael Stillwater and Alan Cohen
Joy is my Compass

How much joy do you allow yourself to feel each day? Two minutes? One hour?

What we need to do is realize that we are children of God and then let that realization overflow into our work, our pastimes and our conversations.

Are there necessary, tiresome chores that you can't seem to find any joy in doing—chores such as laundry, dusting, cleaning bathrooms or the garage? Take those tasks and think of them as "sacred rituals." Then let the indwelling spirit of God take over.

As a child of the Beloved, I can choose to remain joyful in spite of a seeming lack or limitation in my life. I merely adjust my thinking and connect with Infinite Joy.

Spirit is a constant waterfall of happiness. The more joy I express, the more that waterfall of bliss cascades down and through my life.

Affirmation: Today, I let joy be my compass.

NAMASTE

February 9
Choices

"Two roads diverged in a wood, and I took the one less traveled . . ."
-Robert Frost

God has given us the free will to choose how we want to live our lives each and every day.

Normally those choices are based on our thoughts and beliefs. I am not making the same choices that I made twenty or thirty years ago, because my opinions and principles have changed.

The more I recognize Spirit Within, the more I find myself choosing only those thoughts and beliefs that heighten my own right-thinking—my own good.

Since the Universe always says "yes" to my beliefs and my thoughts, I strive to keep those thoughts and beliefs positive and loving . . . sometimes even humorous. (I think God loves to laugh!)

If what I have chosen for my life doesn't seem to be working, whether it be a bad relationship, moving to another town or even what to wear or what to eat, I have only to choose again.

Today, think about your life and what you want it to be and then possibly take steps to choose again.

Affirmation: I can always choose again.

NAMASTE

February 10
An Abundant Life

"He brought us into a place and gave us this land, a land
flowing with milk and honey."
-Deuteronomy 26:9

A teenage boy approached me the other day and asked, "Lady, are you rich?"

My answer was "Yes, I am."

He then said, "Do you live in a big house?"

I laughed and said, "No, I live in a mobile home in a senior park."

He winced. "You say you're rich but you live in a trailer?"

"No," I answered, "I said I was rich and I live in a mobile home—with a very lovely front porch, I might add."

He then asked if I could give him twenty dollars. Well, I knew that the money would probably go to his drug dealer, and so I answered, "No, but I can give you a hug and a promise to pray that God will give you a wonderful, productive life."

He took the hug, lingered to talk for a little longer and then went his merry way.

Our conversation stuck with me over the next week or so and I realized that what I told this young man was true. I am rich—very rich! Even on a "fixed income," I have so much abundance that it flows like the milk and honey in the Old Testament book of Deuteronomy.

My prosperity includes not only my monetary blessings, but the love of a devoted husband and children, other family members and my spiritual family as well.

I am blessed with a home where everyone loves to gather. I have plenty of food to nourish my body and to share with others at the many dinner parties that I host.

Then, of course, there's my furry, little Zen Master, Punkie. She's worth a million dollars to me.

Am I rich? Oh, my, YES! Wealthy beyond words!

Affirmation: Each day, my abundance increases.

NAMASTE

February 11
Web of Life

"Be still, and know that I am God."
-Psalms 46:10

While I rest on my porch this morning with my furry, little Zen-Master beside me, I gaze at a spider sitting in her dew-covered web after a night of spinning.

It's one of God's miracles to me to see the intricate design of a spider's work. It took me years to perfect the art of crochet and yet, in a single night, this Spirit-made creature fabricated a glorious web—a web perfect in its symmetry and grace. And every inch of it was spun solely on her innate knowing. She merely used the mind of God and co-created.

We could all learn from that spider—learn to simply go within and listen to the still, small voice of God and follow the Beloved's lead. How much richer and more creative our lives would be if we would but "Be still and know."

Affirmation: Today I listen to that still, small voice and create a perfect web.

NAMASTE

February 12
Inward Peace

"Calm soul of all things! Make it mine to feel amid the city's jar,
That there abides a peace of Thine,
Man did not make, and cannot mar."
-Matthew Arnold

As we gaze down into a body of water ruffled by the winds, it reflects a distorted picture of who we really are.

Much the same happens when we are confused, distraught or ill. It is at these times that we need to quiet our minds—calm the waters, so to speak, and let the tranquility of that Higher Power subdue and still our lives so that the distortion, once again, becomes pure and clear.

Affirmation: I claim the stillness of God and feel a deep and abiding inward peace.

NAMASTE

February 13
The Power of Gravitation

"The gravitational force of God lovingly moves me in the right direction."
-Author

Just as we experience the power of gravitational force, holding us in place, we can also use it in a spiritual sense. Webster's Dictionary defines gravitation as, "The force of attraction between any two masses," and "A movement or tendency toward something or someone."

When we move toward the gravitational force of God, we are held in place by the force of a Sustaining Power, a loving attraction between us and All That Is.

Affirmation: I am held in the gravitational force of the Beloved.

NAMASTE

February 14
Love

"One word frees us of all the weight and pain of life: that word is love."
-Sophocles

Today is Valentine's Day, a day set aside for love. Don't you just adore the word "love?" It flows from our lips and our hearts and then out to the Universe like a single-word ballad.

It thrills me to know that God in me is love; therefore, I am love.

How much faster we heal when those who cherish us gather around our beds, speaking in affectionate tones! How dear to us is a bouquet of flowers or a box of luscious chocolates sent by a cherished friend or lover?

Yes, today is Valentine's Day, but each and everyday is a day of love!

HAPPY VALENTINE'S DAY!

Affirmation: I will make every day a day of love.

NAMASTE

Look Around You and Within You

"Beauty is the gift of God."
-Aristotle

It is now dusk and from my front porch I have a view of the snow-capped San Gabriel Mountains, as well as the spectacle of a clump of white, papery narcissus and a regal, red poinsettia blooming in my garden. The trees, now bare of leaves, promise an abundance of spring blush and the green-leafed, winter gardenia emits a sweet, delicate aroma.

How lovely is the palette of God's sunset colors, how sweet the face of a graceful pansy, and the fragrance of a last-blooming rose.

Recognizing that God is the very essence of this landscape and the essence of me as well, brings a feeling of wholeness, beauty and peace.

Affirmation: I see Divine Beauty in everything around me.

NAMASTE

February 16
We Create From the Mind of God

"The primary imagination I hold to be the living power and prime agent of all human perception . . . .the finite mind of the eternal act of creation in the infinite I Am."
-Samuel Taylor Coleridge

When we wake in the middle of the night with an idea for a new invention, a solution of an ongoing problem, words to a tune we have composed or an outline for an entire book, we are merely projecting from the creativity of the Great Thinker.

How delightful to see ourselves as instruments through which the Beloved plays out our individual destiny—that portion of life that is ours alone to create through the Divine Mind of God in us.

Affirmation: I create all things with the help of the Ultimate Creator.

NAMASTE

Flawed Or Fabulous?

"We are all here to express the perfection of our
higher, beautiful selves."
-Author

How many of us bemoan the fact that we are seemingly imperfect? Maybe we don't meet the "skinny" standard of a model or perhaps we are physically or, in some other way, challenged.

Let me share with you a story by, once again, my favorite author, "Unknown."

"A water bearer had two large pots, one hung on each end of a pole which he carried across his neck. One of the pots had a crack in it, while the other pot was perfect and always delivered a full portion of water.

"At the end of the long walk from the stream to the master's house, the cracked pot always arrived half full. For two years this went on daily, with the bearer delivering one and a half pots of water to the master's house. Of course, the perfect pot was proud of its accomplishments, fulfilled in the design for which it was made. But the poor cracked pot was ashamed of its own imperfection, and unhappy that it was unable to accomplish what it had been created to do.

"After two years of enduring this bitter shame, the pot spoke to the water bearer one day by the stream. 'I have been able, for these past two years, to deliver only half my load because this crack in my side causes water to leak out all the way back to your master's house. Because of my flaws, you have to do all of this work, and you don't get full value from your efforts,' the pot said.

"The water bearer felt sorry for the old cracked pot, and in his compassion he said, 'As we return to the master's house, I want you to notice the beautiful flowers along the path.' Indeed, as they went up the hill, the old cracked pot took notice of the sun warming the beautiful wild flowers on the side of the path and was cheered somewhat. But at the end of the trail, it still felt the old shame because it had leaked out half its load, and so, again, the pot apologized to the bearer for its failure.

"The bearer said to the pot, 'Did you not notice that there were flowers on your side of the path, and not on the other pot's side? That's because I have always known about your flaw, and I took advantage of it. I planted flower seeds on your side of the path, and every day while we've walked back from the stream, you've watered them. For two years I have been able to pick these beautiful flowers to decorate my master's table. Without you being just the way you are, he would not have this beauty to grace his house.'

"Each of us has what we may term 'flaws,' however, nothing is wasted. Don't be afraid of your flaws or mistakes. Accept them, acknowledge them, use them, and you, too, will bring something beautiful to this world."

Affirmation: I accept the beauty that I bring to this world.

NAMASTE

February 18

What if?

"If we put a positive spin to "what is" in our lives, we can
eliminate the "what ifs."
-Author

The two small words, "what if," can keep us from living a full and
productive life.

What if I lose my job?

What if I become ill?

What if my house burns down and I lose everything?

What if my children don't live up to my expectations?

What if my husband leaves me?

"What if" is a game where everyone loses. It keeps us from living
in the present, from enjoying every beautiful, sacred moment that the
Beloved has to offer.

The past is over, the future is unknown, but the present—ah, the
present is a gift to be cherished.

Affirmation: I give up my "what ifs" for the joy of "what is."

NAMASTE

February 19
All the World's a Stage

"If all the world's a stage, I want to dance on every square inch of it."
-Author

Think back on your life at the many roles you have played, the numerous masks you have worn. You've cried through tragedies and soared like an eagle in times of ecstasy. You've trembled from stage fright and wanted to hide behind the curtain of life during times of grief.

We wear so many masks, each one changing with our circumstances and challenges.

In her class workbook, Dancing with Spirit, Nancy Nisonger writes:

"Whether you have chosen to be the star, or an extra, the question is—does it really matter? Of all the masks we wear and roles we play, when we stop pretending and become our authentic selves, we now gain awareness and act as co-creator with our Higher Power. That means, whichever role we are playing is absolutely the right one for us at that time. We can be whatever we want to be—producer, director, diva, extra, stage center, or behind the scenes. The choice is ours."

Get out on that stage! Dance in the spotlight! "Break a leg!"

Affirmation: Today I'll choose my role and play it well.

NAMASTE

February 20
I Can Grow

"Highly functioning people say, "Where I am is fine, but I can grow."
-Dr. Wayne Dyer
Everyday Wisdom for Success

What would you like to do that you have never done before?

I started writing seriously at the age of sixty-five. Being an avid reader, I was always fascinated by the written word and how magically the authors could string these words together and come up with intriguing stories and lyrical poems. I have now published a novel and hope to complete more books in the future.

It's never too late to grow.

Affirmation: Today I will do something I have never done before.

NAMASTE

February 21
Let Go!

"On with the dance!
Let Joy be unconfined."
-Lord Byron

Recently my husband and I attended a ceremony that ended with a wild frenzy of dancing. The music grabbed my soul and as I watched my friends "tripping" across the floor, my feet literally took on a life of their own.

I found myself completely lost inside my own heart's rhythm as I danced with my adopted twelve-year-old grandson and his father, then flew around the dance floor all by myself.

How freeing it is to let go of our inhibitions, to forget our prim and proper upbringings and—DANCE!

Affirmation: Today I unshackle my inhibitions and dance with the Universe.

NAMASTE

February 22

Simply Being

"Rest in the moment."
-Author

The tap, tap of rain against my bedroom window serves as a rhythmic reminder that today I wish to indulge in quiet introspection, meditation and reading.

I've brought a cup of tea and one of my many spiritual books to my bed. Punkie has scratched herself a nesting place among the blankets and we both breathe out a gentle sigh of comfort.

I have nowhere I must be and nothing urgent to do. I have only the present moment—only the satisfaction of that lovely, blessed present moment.

How pleasant it is to allow ourselves those times of "simply being."

Affirmation: Today I will indulge myself with tea and stillness.

NAMASTE

February 23
Clarity and Illumination

"Stepping away from a situation brings clarity and illumination."
-Author

How many times have we been unclear as to what our decisions should be? It's as though we're wearing someone else's glasses and everything is fuzzy.

To become clear, we need to step outside of ourselves, to let go of needing to force something, in order to get the bigger, more focused picture. It is then that we become "decision illuminated," throwing light on the problem-at-hand.

When we clear our minds and slip into prayer and meditation, we start seeing with a new set of eyes. We become "observers" as we ask "What is meaningful here? What is there to learn that I am not seeing or understanding?" Illuminating moments come when we can ask and then answer these questions through that Still, Small Voice within.

When we live in the space of "illumination," we find our answers and find, also, the joy of this journey called "life."

Affirmation: I will get clarity in knowing what to do and live in the brilliance of God.

NAMASTE

February 24
Constantly Realigning

"We truly are all one. It is encoded in our cells and in our souls."
-Author

Quantum physics shows us, at a subatomic level, that we are all one. In research labs, when researchers chemically separate crystal particles, those same particles waste no time quickly realigning themselves, of their own accord, to point in the same original direction.

This interconnectedness is encoded in our cells as well. An experiment was done where college students watched a movie of Mother Theresa helping the poor. The immune systems of these students greatly improved. It was so even for those who scoffed at the movie.

We are definitely all brothers and sisters, who, like the crystal particles, are constantly realigning ourselves in love.

Affirmation: I am one with all of life and with that all sustaining Divine Intelligence.

NAMASTE

The Lord is My Shepherd

"The Lord is my shepherd, I shall not want. He maketh me to lie down in green pastures; he leadeth me beside the still waters."
-Psalms 23:1 & 2

Clouds circle the mountains like thick smoke this morning, hiding their magnificence and splendor. But, like God, although unseen, their majesty and strength still do exist.

We may not be able to "see" the Beloved, but He is there nevertheless. We catch glimpses of Him in a fragrant red rose, a graceful pine tree, a great blue heron and in the eyes of a tiny newborn.

Mostly, He is with us waiting to be acknowledged so that He can lead us through every step of our lives. And, sometimes, when we need God most, He lifts us into His loving arms and carries us over the rough terrain.

Affirmation: I am safe and protected in God's love.

NAMASTE

February 26

Conscious Living

"I yam what I yam."
-Popeye

Every moment of our lives we walk on a sacred path, and, as we travel, it is important to ask ourselves, "What is the purpose of my journey?"

Maybe it would be important to first discover the core of who we truly are.

Over the years we've been told who we are by our parents, our peers, our teachers and our religious leaders. But who are we, really?

When we can recognize that at the hub of our being is a Sacred Entity, a loving God who can help us erase all of the negative things that we have been told we are, give us a clean slate, then we can start loving ourselves, recognizing who we really are.

Reintroduce yourself to yourself. Talk about what a wonderful person you are.

Each day appreciate yourself a little more. Find out where your happiness lies. Figure out for yourself how you want to worship your Higher Power. Allow that wonderful you to be who you are. Then, and only then, will you discover the true purpose of your life.

Affirmation: I will become conscious of who I really am and walk my sacred path.

NAMASTE

The Extension of God's Love

"When the soul breathes through a man's intellect, it is genius;
when it breaks through his will, it is virtue; when it flows
through his affection, it is love."
-Ralph Waldo Emerson

The Beloved shows His love to us in so many ways. He offers us the beauty of each new day, the song of the morning birds, the splash of a bubbling brook and the magnificence of towering mountains.

He loves us through our mates, our families and our friends and even, sometimes, through perfect strangers who smile as we pass on the sidewalk.

Our all-knowing, all-giving God shows us affection in every way He can.

Affirmation: Today I look for signs of God's love.

NAMASTE

February 28
Thinking Outside the Box

"Everything has its beauty but not everyone sees it."
-Confucius

Everything is constructed of the same energy. Sound is a denser and slower vibration of light and matter is a denser, slower vibration of sound. Everything is forever alive and moving, expanding and contracting.

Allowing yourself to see life at this level, you can feel everything coming alive. Life lived "out of the box" is beautiful. "The box" keeps us unaware.

As a child, my family traveled extensively. My dad, a military man, was transferred from base to base. I can remember feeling the heaviness of relocation, the emptiness of no "home town." So, as we traveled to each new place, my imagination comforted me while I gazed out of the window of the car, seeing visions of tiny, colorful fairies emerging from flowers and trees along the highway. Those small, imaginary creatures kept my fears from overwhelming me. I thought outside "the box" in order to give myself peace.

Take time today to think outside "the box." See everything as living and breathing—expanding and contracting. Stop and smell the roses if you live in a warm climate, or let the snowflakes fall on your outstretched tongue if you live in a colder area.

Either way, feel the life energy in the roses and the snowflakes. Doing this will give you a new appreciation for everything and for the God who created our magnificent universe.

Affirmation: Today I will think and live outside "the box."

NAMASTE

February 29

Happy Birthday!

"Today might be your birthday—are you twenty or are you eighty?"
-Author

Leap year comes upon us every four years, when the Gregorian calendar (a common solar calendar) compensates for the natural order of the Earth.

The Earth takes 365 days, five hours and forty-eight minutes to revolve around the sun. By the fourth year, we are a bit out-of-sync, and so another day, February 29, is added to make up for the difference.

So rejoice! If today you are turning eighty, my dear, you are only a Gregorian twenty.

Oh, by the way, February 29 is also the year when we women are allowed to propose marriage to our "special guy!"

Affirmation: On this extra day of the year, I will propose to "my guy," even if it's only a proposal to share a meal and a glass of wine.

NAMASTE

March 1

Crystals and Gemstones

"Deep within me lies a place of peace,
An indwelling sanctuary of cool, lavender silence;
And within that holy temple I hear the omniscient center
Of my being—Infinite Voice of Love."
-Author

Tonight I meditated while holding in my hand the violet gemstone, charoite.

Violet is the highest vibrating of all colors. It is also associated with the seventh and highest chakra—the crown chakra.

Holding a gemstone or a crystal in our hand during meditation often heightens our senses and our awareness of God. It can also deepen and enhance the meditative state.

I would like to encourage you to go to a store that carries crystals and gemstones and choose one that calls out to you with its beauty and shape. While you're there, find a book on them. You'll learn how they are formed and how, for thousands of years, they have been valued for their healing powers as well as for their beauty.

The study of these God-created miracles is fascinating as well as informative.

Affirmation: Today I will have a "crystal day," a "gemstone day" of delight and beauty.

NAMASTE

March 2

Creative Cubbyholes

"Joy is having a creative cubbyhole."
-Author

I love to write—to co-create with God. The space allotted to me for this creative endeavor is a former closet that has been turned into a work station. My husband removed the sliding glass doors, took down the hanging bars and built a long, Formica-covered counter top. My computer, printer and miscellaneous files sit nicely on top of this "desk."

Where is this miraculous workspace? In my bathroom!

I sold an article to a magazine and during the course of a telephone conversation with the editor he said, "I'm always curious to know where my contributors do their writing. Some have lofts, some rent office space, while others have a special room in their home. Where do you write, Mrs. Dillon?"

UH OH!!

Without thinking, I blurted out, "In my bathroom." Then, stammering I explained that I lived in a senior mobile home park and that the remodeled closet was the only available space.

After laughing together and chatting a bit longer, we ended our conversation. As I hung up the phone, I realized how very much I loved my work area. It's quiet, my furry Zen-Master, Punkie, can see me from our bed where she now spends most of her old age, and who wants to disturb me when I'm in the bathroom?

It doesn't matter where we are when we create, it only matters that, as

Henry Ward Beecher said, "Happiness lies in the absorption in some vocation which satisfies the soul."

Affirmation: I see my workspace as perfect.

NAMASTE

March 3

Mapping Out Our Lives

"Being a diligent cartographer keeps us on our right path."
-Author

Cartography is the science of map drawing. It uses both design and compilation to complete each diagrammatic representation of a route. Without maps, we would all be wandering around, like Moses, in the wilderness of freeways and side streets.

I like to think of myself as a master cartographer. In the morning, as I lie in bed, my mind starts to design my day. I compile a list of things that I wish to accomplish or places I will be going, then I get up and follow the route that I have planned for myself. Some days I may have drawn my map, only to redraw it. Many of my most delightful times have been the side streets taken—the serendipitous interruptions that, like last-minute changes to my map, have led me from a day of writing to a delightful local craft fair and then out to lunch with a dear friend.

When we are diligent cartographers, our lives always run more smoothly. We waste little time wandering and more time co-creating with the Beloved.

Affirmation: Today I will be a master cartographer.

NAMASTE

March 4

Expressing the Divine

"Every act reveals God and expands His Being."
-Meister Eckhart

If what Meister Eckhart expresses in the quote above is true, then every single thing we do is an expression of God. When a writer writes, God is articulated; when a baby cries, God is definitely amplified; and when an orchid blooms, it shows God's burgeoning beauty. Even when your child brings home an "F" on his or her report card, you can explain to him or her that it is merely "Feedback" from God and his teacher.

Every act in this universe, even the ones we label as "bad" are simply lessons to expand His "Beingness" within us.

Affirmation: Divine Beauty within me creates divine acts through me.

NAMASTE

March 5

Enthusiasm

"Enthusiasm is the glory and hope of the world."
-Bronson Alcott

I love spending time with enthusiastic people—people who understand that life is wonderful because it is a gift from God.

We were put on this earth for a purpose. We have God-given gifts, God-inspired love and a fire within that sparks our passions and our joys.

We are all love and creativity in overflowing expression. Our options are limitless as we open our "enthusiasm valves" and let the flow of our ardor and delight fill our lives.

Ralph Waldo Emerson said, "Nothing great was ever achieved without enthusiasm. The way of life is wonderful; it is abandonment."

Affirmation: My enthusiasm ignites the fire of my creativity and joy.

NAMASTE.

March 6
Oneness

"I am tremoring with the textures of life, nurturing and nourishing the
loving touch of Oneness."
-James Twyman
The Proof

Today I am sitting just outside of my favorite sandwich shop at a table
shaded by a cinnamon-brown-and-autumn-gold-striped umbrella.
I linger over a cup of my favorite tea and enjoy the balmy Southern
California weather with my husband, Bill.

Observing the many people walking by, I think to myself, "You and
I are one." A young man amongst the throng turns and smiles as though
hearing my thoughts. Goose bumps rise on my arms—goose bumps of
joy for the act of soul-connection.

After experiencing what he thought was "mind reading," James
Twyman writes in his book, *The Proof*, "Then one day I had a thought:
It wasn't that I was reading people's minds, but that I was somehow
bypassing the idea of separation, experiencing myself as one with them."

I did not read Mr. Twyman's book until after my experience outside
the sandwich shop, but as I read that paragraph, my lovely goose bumps
returned.

Affirmation: Today I will set aside my critical mind and experience the
joy of Oneness.

NAMASTE

March 7
Abundance

I throw out my statements of limitation and speak only
of my abundance."
-Author

It is time to break through the limitation of false restraints—of the depressing feeling of limit. We need, instead, to be aware of God's unlimited abundance, energy and joy.

Lack and deprivation are words we inherited from our parents, the evening news and the "suits" on Wall Street.

God only perceives abundance!

During the darkest time of the recession, my monthly statements from my investments showed a constant minus. I don't touch that money anyway, so I merely put a perpendicular line through the minus sign and made it a plus.

WOW! That worked.

We need to remember, too, that prosperity is not just about money. Abundance is the family that we love and who love us, a quiet afternoon of reading and contemplation, a walk in a park and so many other things. But, most of all, our riches lie in the care of the Beloved, for God only knows abundance—He is our abundance.

Affirmation: Today I see and feel nothing but abundance.

NAMASTE

Women's History Month

"We, as women, are capable of changing the landscape of history."
-Author

In 1987, Congress proclaimed that the month of March would be National Women's History Month, with the purpose of "writing women back into history."

As I am penning this vignette, it is March 8, 2010, and last night another woman made history. Kathryn Bigelow received an Academy Award for best director for the movie, *The Hurt Locker*. She is the first female director to win this prestigious award.

There are so many beautiful female souls who, over the years, have helped to forge our great country. Some have managed to turn history around, making it legal for women to vote, to attend college and even to run for public office.

We've come a long way, ladies, and there is no doubt we will travel even farther.

What part of your own personal history would you like to write? Maybe you've been thinking of changing careers or perhaps you feel your biological clock is ticking and you yearn to experience motherhood. In the allure and awe of this ideal moment, do that which has been calling to you, and, who knows? You just might change the landscape of history.

Affirmation: I am a woman of strength, capable of changing the annals of time.

NAMASTE

It's the Journey That Counts

"Slow down for a more delightful journey."
-Author

Over the past few years, it has become a goal of mine, an aspiration, to be both a published author and to weigh 105 pounds. Don't gasp at the weight, I'm only four feet, eleven inches tall, and, might I add—shrinking. So, you see, 105 pounds is definitely within reason for my height and small bone structure.

Writing a book and losing the pounds are pilgrimages that are interesting and challenging at the same time. I want, however, to do both in a week!

That's definitely not happening!

When we are eager to accomplish something, we often lose sight of enjoying the time it takes to get there in our pursuit to reach the goal.

I am now endeavoring to write my book and change my eating habits with ease and grace, meandering down the path instead of running head-on and stumbling along the way.

If you find yourself overly eager to reach a goal, remember that getting there—the journey—is truly just as important as the end result. Slow down as you savor each moment of your pilgrimage.

Affirmation: In reaching my goal, I will take pleasure in the journey.

NAMASTE

March 10
Pleasure

"Where your pleasure is, there is your treasure: where your treasure,
there your heart; where your heart, there your happiness."
-Saint Augustine

PLEASURE   is listening to the music of life.
PLEASURE   is an Easter egg hunt.
PLEASURE   is waking up to the song of a bird.
PLEASURE   is one coke and two straws.
PLEASURE   is a brand new box of crayons.
PLEASURE   is a just-born litter of puppies.
PLEASURE   is an orange tree fragrant with white blossoms.
PLEASURE   is the smell of baking bread.
PLEASURE   is chocolate in any form.
PLEASURE   is writing this book and sharing it with you.

Affirmation: Today I will look around and discover my own pleasures.

NAMASTE

March 11
Potential Perfection

"God indwells everything which He creates."
-Reverend Danell Wheeler

We are all potentially perfect. Our free choice, however, sometimes takes from that unrealized perfection.

What we need to remember is that we are all divine, perfect, whole and complete, to recognize that Divine Essence within us every moment of every day.

God exists in all of us. His nature is a part of our very makeup. It's up to us to identify with that Indwelling Spirit and to live with purpose and love.

When we accept our God-given perfections, we can then go out into the world embracing our divinity and expressing our humanity.

Affirmation: I recognize that God-in-me is my divine heritage.

NAMASTE

March 12
We Are Never Separated From God

"Beside the river stands the holy tree of life. There doth my father dwell and my home is in him. The heavenly father and I are one."
-The Essence Gospel of Peace

There is in each and every one of us a piece of God. Some call it our souls, some our sacred light and others an individual expression of the One.

As the result of "free will," we often forget that we are spiritual beings walking this earth and we spin downward into the darkness of separation. Then we remember, once again, who we are and spiral back up to our knowingness.

The pain of forgetfulness and the false separation from the Beloved cannot be endured for long. God's unconditional love is waiting until, once again, we remember who we are.

Affirmation: Daily I will remember that the Heavenly Father and I are one.

NAMASTE

March 13
Lighting the Fire Within

"The spark of the Almighty within me awaits to explode into full flame."
-Author

In science there is a theory that combustion will self-ignite at a low temperature. It will occur through oxidation or fermentation. Then, even without the aid of a match, a spontaneous act of fire will occur.

We can touch off a similar flame simply by, moment to moment, awakening to the Divine Within.

The Beloved awaits our recognition of Him and then that recognition can burst into flames of love, creativity, passion for our purpose and desire for peace.

By igniting that Spark within us, we can collectively set the world on fire.

Affirmation: I recognize and use that Fire within me.

NAMASTE

March 14
One Trunk, Many Branches

"The Infinite Trunk of Life holds many branches."
-Author

How many faiths are there in the world? I believe the answer to that question is "as many as man has a need for." My belief is that whatever way you choose to worship is the right way for you. Deep within me I know that there is a golden thread joining us all, and that brilliant cord is God.

Reverend Margaret Stortz, author of *Lights Along the Way*, and minister and practitioner with the Church of Religious Science, recently wrote, "If unity with God and all life is to have any meaning, it must be that the divine senses that we value in ourselves must be present in others . . .Being one religion as contrasted with another does not make one more spiritual than another. We are all imbued with as much God as we will ever be; it simply remains for us to uncover that "God-ness." . . . . Once we allow others the expectations we have for ourselves— health, happiness, self-expression, love interest—we can stop judging them. We may not know of their individual hopes and dreams, but we can know them as nestled in the heart of God as we are, awakening to their own senses of spirituality in the ways that are right for them."

Affirmation: I see the love of God in all faiths.

NAMASTE

March 15

Ahh, the Good Life

"The actuality of thought is life."
-Aristotle

For me, living the good life includes sitting and meditating on my front porch; sharing meals with my friends and family and co-creating with the Beloved.

For you, it might mean going to a job that you love each day, traveling to far-off countries, or, perhaps, owning your own business.

Spirit will never interfere with our choices. He allows us to pick what we will or will not experience.

How exciting to know that we can select a full and busy life or a slow and casual pace. Either way, Infinite Mind will accept whatever life we love and want. God always honors us to the degree of our own imaginations and expectations.

Affirmation: I am thankful for the life I have chosen.

NAMASTE

March 16
Thanks for Nothing!

"Dolce far niente!"
-Old Italian saying

The translation of the above old Italian saying is: "How sweet it is to do nothing."

I sat in my sanctuary this morning for three hours doing just that—NOTHING!

Now, through the open windows, a whispering breeze moves the lace curtains ever so gently. And, outside, on the front porch overhang, a basket filled with pink, red and white petunias rocks languidly to-and-fro.

Scattered moments of deep contemplation, followed by larger intervals of quiet meditation have occupied my time, but, mostly, I have been doing nothing. And, through this, I am savoring a rapturous peace—the tranquil serenity of "nothingness."

Affirmation: I will take time for the peacefulness of *dolce far niente*.

NAMASTE

March 17
Quirky Words

"Life is a metaphor of quirky words and whimsical characters."
-Author

When my son was three and four years old, he loved the book, Green Eggs and Ham. Over time, having memorized the book, I could close my eyes and know exactly when to turn the page.

Theodor Geisel, known to all of us as Dr. Seuss, wrote fanciful, worthwhile messages that included an elephant that hatched eggs and cats that wore hats.

There is great power in our imaginations. Sometimes, however, through the everyday structure of life, we forget to have fun—to be playful with our words.

Let your mind open to that whimsical part of you and, who knows, you just might discover purple and orange zebras and mules that fly.

Affirmation: I do so love goofy words and fun
Thank you for them, Infinite One.

NAMASTE

March 18
Waiting

"In waiting, we must resort to both patience and detachment."
-Author

T.S. Eliot wrote, "Hurry up please, it's time."

As women, we have learned the art of waiting—we wait until we are old enough to wear makeup—to have double piercings—to date—to leave home for college—to have that "can't live without him" guy propose. Then, there's the nine months it takes to bring new life into the world. And the list goes on.

I have a dear friend, who, along with her husband, has purchased a home—it's what they call a "short sale." EXCUSE ME? Where did they come up with that term? It seems to be taking eons longer than if it had been a "long sale."

I asked her if the wait wasn't driving her crazy and she answered "I distract myself. I get regular massages, I take classes, I buy jewelry; actually, I simply detach from the whole thing. I put things into perspective. After all, I have my health, the love of family and friends, and a place to live. I have it all, anyway, so what is there to be impatient about?"

Now, here is a woman who has learned that waiting is merely the time between the dream and the culmination of that dream. It is the journey toward it while continuing to live her beautiful life. It is detaching.

Affirmation: I dream, I detach, and I wait with immeasurable grace.

NAMASTE

March 19

Memories

Their very memory is fair and bright. . ."
-Henry Vaughan

Reach out today and touch the texture and weave of a past enjoyable memory. Feel it deep within. Relive the taste, the smell and the sound of that gentle recollection.

Some of my most cherished memories are the times spent with my grandchildren: Jenny and Joey coming to stay with Grandma and Grandpa; the board games played with Katie and Chanse; the motor home trips with Kellene; the Holidays, parties and lunches with Nick and Noelle; Christmases with Austin, Thea and Nathan; and loving visits with Steven and Jennifer. Then, there is the day that Bill's granddaughter, Jade, first called me "Grandma." How dear are these grandchildren, how precious the memories that linger on.

Through our memories, our senses whisper the longing of our souls—bring us to those places of ascendancy and renewal.

Today, revisit that lovely, long-ago experience and any other beautiful moments in your life that you can recall.

When, in our minds, we roll those sacred moments around and around, like sweet chocolate morsels, we encourage ourselves to revel in our senses, to feel, hear and taste those fair and bright memories.

Affirmation: Today I will relive the happy times of my past while weaving into the tapestry of my life, more beautiful, transcendent moments.

NAMASTE

March 20
Celebrating Nature

"Happiness is a garden—your own small piece of heaven-on-earth."
-Author

Because today began as an exceptionally warm one for March, I donned my "grubby" clothes and my worn "tennies" and ventured outside to work in the garden.

It was three sun-drenched hours of weeding, assisting my husband in placing stepping stones from my arbor to my front porch, and visiting with neighbors out for their morning strolls.

I stopped periodically to look around, enjoying the lovely garden creation—the small bit of heaven-on-earth where God has placed me.

John Milton expressed my own feelings so perfectly when he wrote:

"In those vernal seasons of the year when the air is calm and pleasant, it were an injury and sullenness against nature not to go out and see her riches, and partake in her rejoicing with heaven and earth."

RIGHT ON, MR. MILTON!

Affirmation: On the next warm day, I will venture outside to enjoy the riches of nature.

NAMASTE

March 21
A Stroll Along the Pathway of Life

"My path leads toward enlightenment."
-Author

Just as losing weight and writing this book are journeys, so, too, is spiritual growth, or what Buddhists call "the pathway to enlightenment."

The practice of spiritual enlightenment takes a lifetime or, who knows, perhaps many lifetimes.

I picture myself strolling along a broad, unending path, picking the exotic flowers of the truth as I see it, feeling the presence of the Beloved walking beside me, guiding me over the stones and uphill slopes that invariably show up along the way.

Spiritual growth is an individual experience—a subtle happening within the privacy of each individual soul.

I walk along the sacred path of life,
Listening to the words my soul contains.
A journey filled with joy and sometimes strife,
A metaphor of minuses and gains.
-Author

Affirmation: Today I walk the sacred path of the truth as I see it.

NAMASTE

March 22
Yin and Yang

"The combined essences of heaven and earth become the yin and yang, the concentrated essences of the yin and yang become the four seasons, and the scattered essences of the four seasons become the myriad creatures of the world."
-Huai-nan Tzu

Each person has within them both female and male aspects. It is the duality of the Chinese philosophy of yin and yang.

The yin, or female part of us, is the deepest, wisest portion of who we are. It is the perceptive, sensitive side of us—the receiving end through which the universe can flow. The yin portion of us is intuitive, communicating through the inner voice—that place of deep knowing.

The yang, or male aspect of ourselves is all about endeavor— the doing, the action. It is the out flowing end of the channel—the performance segment of us.

The Yin receives the thought, the energy of creation and the yang takes it out into the world.

It is through the energies of both that the creative process exists.

Affirmation: I possess the duality of both the yin and the yang.

NAMASTE

March 23
We Only Have Today

"But today well lived makes every yesterday a dream of happiness, and every tomorrow a vision of hope. Look well therefore to this day! Such is the salutation of the dawn!"
-Sanskrit poem
Author unknown

We only have today. Let that be enough.

Enjoy the gentle delights of day-to-day living. Erase the yesterdays and the tomorrows so that "hope can spring eternal" for just this one, twenty-four hour period.

Feel the dance of the moment from the time you arise to the tucking of yourself between the sheets at night.

Discover Spirit in everyone you see, in the radiance of the morning sun, the tulip bulbs poking through the rich earth, the red-flowering of the pomegranate tree. Sit and watch the grass grow or take a one-day train ride to an antique mall in the next county. Or, possibly, start writing a novel.

There are so many wondrous things to do in just one day.

Affirmation: Today I will fill each precious moment.

NAMASTE

March 24
Letting Go of Fear

"Fear comes from not trusting the process of life to be there for you."
-Louise L. Hay
Heart Thoughts

I am sleeping. Suddenly I wake up. It is the middle of the night. I am experiencing awesome, unknown fear.

When apprehension strikes in the darkness of night, my mind automatically turns to a litany of affirmations that never fail to calm me. I whisper them to myself: "Be still and know that I am God;" "I am safe;" "I am divinely and lovingly protected."

Make up your own affirmations or mantras and when awakened by fearful thoughts, repeat them over and over.

Affirmation: In times of fear I will affirm my safety.

NAMASTE

Ego Versus Infinite Awareness

"The ego likes little boxes it is familiar with. But when considering an infinite consciousness, the first thing you have to do is burn the boxes."
-Stuart Wilde
Infinite Self
33 Steps To Reclaiming Your Inner Power

Our ever-present egos have the persistent knack of getting in the middle of the path toward our higher awareness. We need to take out the "I/me" concept of ego and reach inward to that "I Am" place—that place of the God Within.

When we humble ourselves to the fact that Infinite Life dwells in everything and everyone, we can burn those "ego boxes" that Mr. Wilde speaks of and spend the rest of our lives on the path of discovering our "Infinite Selves."

Affirmation: Today I will recognize the Infinite Consciousness within me.

NAMASTE

March 26
The Winds of Time

"He rode upon a cherub, and did fly: yea, he did fly upon
the wings of the wind."
-Psalms 18:10

The winds are strong this morning. The newly-sprouted leaves on the limbs of the camphor trees whip about in a reckless, frenzied dance.

Punkie and I sit huddled on the front porch swing, she wrapped snuggly in her green, fuzzy "blankie," while I cozy myself in a multi-colored quilt.

The currents of air today are sometimes tempestuous, squalling gusts that periodically change to a light, breezy ballet of wispy, soft air.

Over the years, the metaphoric winds of time bring both turbulence and gentle breezes into our lives. But, like Punkie and me, nestled in our blankets, through the squalls and zephyrs of life, we are always and forever shielded under the cloak of the Infinite Protector.

Affirmation: Through the winds of time I am always protected.

NAMASTE

March 27
The Four Archangels

"Therefore with Angels and Archangels, and with all the company of heaven, we laud and magnify thy glorious name; evermore praising thee."

-The Book of Common Prayer

From an Ancient, mystical Jewish Prayer:

"I call on the four archangels to encircle me:

I invoke URIEL in front of me. He is the angel of clarity and discrimination.

Uriel, please clear my mind. Help me have a clear vision, a pure heart and wise discrimination.

I call for MICHAEL to be on my right side. He is the angel of love and loving kindness. Michael, please show me how to open my heart in true loving kindness, especially when I am not feeling loving at all. Help me to graciously accept your love and the love of others. Help me to love myself, others and the world. Flow through me please.

I invoke the angel GABRIEL on my left side. He brings strength and helps overcome fear. Gabriel, take from me my many fears. In each fearful situation hold me close and enfold me in your powerful wings. I take your strength as my own and thank you for it.

Behind me is RAPHAEL. He is the angel of healing. Raphael, I ask for your healing. I ask that you care for the healings of those others in need right now. I ask you to move into my body, permeating all of my being with your healing energy.

I ask the four of you to allow your love to flow into my heart and then out to others who are in need of help and blessing.

Archangels Uriel, Michael, Gabriel and Raphael love to answer when I call. I am encircled by angelic love."

Affirmation: I take this ancient, mystical Jewish prayer as my own.

NAMASTE

March 28
Soundless Love

"Looking into your eyes and seeing the sparkle of light that springs from your center to speak wordlessly to mine."
-Renee Potter

Some of my most profound moments of love have occurred when, without words, my eyes have met with another's, igniting such a bright flame of passion that it caused my heart to open simply through that gazing love.

My husband's eyes are of such a blue that the oceans of his caring seem to pour into me like the thundering waves of the rolling seas.

Then there is my furry Zen Master, Punkie; she has lost most of her ability to hear and so, more and more, she is relying on her eyes to communicate. Over the years, each morning, I have said to her, "Punkie, I love you like a rock!" She always wriggled with joy when I emphasized the word "rock." Now she stares at me as I speak our morning ritual words, knowing without hearing what I am saying and through our eye connection, she continues to wriggle with joy.

Let us all feel that connection of love through the sparkle of light that springs from our centers.

Affirmation: Today I will look through and into the eyes of love.

NAMASTE

The Art of Non Attachment

"If we 'let go' of being attached to something, we can
then 'let go' and just be."
-Author

This morning from my front porch I can see a long-tailed, scaly lizard resting in a torpid state on the sun-drenched driveway.

I would like to think that he is practicing the art of "non attachment." It's not that he is unengaged in life nor uncaring of his world, he is simply warming his little back and following one of the ancient Buddhist teachings that the greatest joy comes from "a mind that clings to naught."

Through detachment, we too can rest peacefully in the warm sunlight of "letting go." Like the lizard on my driveway, we can learn not to define ourselves by our attachments.

What are some of the things that we attach ourselves to? It could be a person, a cause, money, or, perhaps, social status. As long as we permit our avid desires to possess us, we will never experience the true serenity of a fulfilling life.

We don't need to rid ourselves of our desires. They are not the problem. It is our attachment to these things that are the stumbling blocks along our path to enlightenment.

It is a simple, and sometimes not so simple, matter of just "letting go."

William Blake wrote:

"He who binds to himself a joy

Does the winged life destroy;

But he who kisses the joy as it flies

Lives in eternity's sunrise."

Affirmation: I will develop a mind that clings to nothing.

NAMASTE

March 30
Hi, Old Friend

"The later years of our life are to be the years of our greatest treasures."
-Louise L. Hay
Experience Your Good Now!

The diary of my life is written in the lines on my face, the smocked skin on my legs and arms, the crinkly burrows between my eyes and the whitening of my hair. Each recorded page is scribed with the evidence of time.

Yet, when I gaze into a mirror, it is like seeing an old and faithful friend. A close companion who, hand-in-hand, has shared with me magical journeys and intriguing adventures. That perfect friend whose unconditional love flows from the Magnificent Source within her.

Affirmation: Today, I will look in the mirror and discover my best friend.

NAMASTE

Have a Good Cry

"It opens the lungs, washes the countenance, exercises the eyes, and softens down the temper, so cry away."
-Charles Dickens

When we cry, we open up the floodgates of sadness, anger and, sometimes, even joy.

How many of our parents said to us, "Stop that or I'll really give you something to cry about?" Well, guess what? If we were crying we obviously felt we had something to cry about. Tell me, just how much sense did those words of our parents make?

Or, maybe, they said, "Big boys don't cry." Oh yeah? Have you ever watched the individual faces of a football team that just won the Super Bowl? More tears have been shed on a football field than can be counted. Now, you can't find boys any bigger and heartier than those shoulder-padded giants.

For me, crying comes with each deeply felt emotion: a song that touches my soul, a harsh word from someone I love and even a special, unexpected gift will start me weeping. Heck, lately all I have to do is watch a Hallmark commercial on television and I'm running for a box of tissues.

The poet, Heinrich Heine, wrote, "Whatever tears one sheds, in the end one always blows one's nose."

Affirmation: As tears run down my cheeks, they wash my psyche and my soul.

NAMASTE

April 1

Happy All Fools' Day

"This fellow's wise enough to play the fool, and to do that well craves a kind of wit."
William Shakespeare

Today is April Fools' Day—a day of practical jokes and lightheartedness. It is a day when we can turn that cultured, refined adult into a delightful, impish child.

As you observe this fun-loving day, dance with Spirit while playing your pranks and mischievous capers. Bury a pair of tickets to the basketball game that you have wrapped in foil under your husband's toast, put a small toy inside the shoe of that "special kid" in your life or maybe tell your mother you're taking her to "Aunt Sue's" and then drive her to a day spa for an April Fools' massage. Maybe you can think of something a little more devilish, like short-sheeting your kids' beds, or, if it's raining on April the first, put some confetti into your husband's umbrella, close it and wait for him to open it. Maybe cutting off all of the bristles on a toothbrush would be fun. Just be sure you have an extra in the bathroom cupboard.

Experience the unsophisticated, innocent delights of that youngster within you. Doing so, just might link you to a significant hidden aspect of yourself.

Affirmation: This will be a day of practical jokes and fun.

NAMASTE

April 2
Dancing With Spirit

"We're fools whether we dance or not, so we might as well dance."
-Japanese proverb

Too often, I find myself absorbed in the preoccupation of everyday life. I lose touch with that "dancer" within me, forgetting what gleeful fun it is to move in rhythmic ecstasy—to feel the freedom and joy of reconnecting with my Inner Flowing Spirit.

Soooo—last week I took a class. I learned how to dance the Salsa!

Now, "salsa" is the Spanish word for sauce—a spicy flavor. And, boy, did we get "spicy" with our moves!

Salsa music ranges from 150 to 250 beats per minute and includes using your hips—the famous "Cuban hip movement." (I knew there was a reason for that ample part of my body.)

The class lasted for almost two hours and this old gal went home with a slight limp and a smile so bright she hardly needed the headlights on her car!

When we allow that music within us to partner-up with the Beloved Dancer of our Souls, we soon learn to follow where He leads.

Affirmation: Today I will dance with Spirit.

NAMASTE

April 3
From Darkness to Light

"Out of darkness springs new life."
-Author

This morning, outside of my living room window, I'm watching two Mallard ducks, a drake and a hen, waddle toward my garden. It's April, the month of mating for these feathered creatures, and I know that "Mama" is searching for a place to lay her eggs. I can only hope that, this year, she chooses to make her nest underneath my flowering pomegranate tree.

In past years, I have witnessed the hatching of many ducklings, watching as those feathery babies worked to peck their way from darkness into the light of new life.

How many other living things must go through darkness in order to emerge into the light?

When we plant a bulb in the ground, it must first grow through the dense soil before it blossoms out into the sunlight. A butterfly, too, must evolve within a dark cocoon before it can break free and fly away.

Sometimes, we, as human beings, experience cocoons of temporary darkness—addiction, illness or the loss of a loved one, to name but a few. Not unlike the duck, the caterpillar and the bulb, we, too, can emerge from these places into the light of growth and understanding. With the help of the Beloved, we can choose to transform into what we truly are—whole, perfect and complete.

Affirmation: Today I find my way out of the dark and into the light of wholeness.

NAMASTE

April 4

Hey! It's Time to Play!

"At the age of seventy-six, I play more now than
I did when I was sixteen."
-Author

We always think of play as something only a child does.

NOT TRUE!

As we get older, responsibilities take over our lives—working, raising children, paying bills—these things replace our childlike qualities and make us forget the "fun" parts of ourselves.

So, when do we get to "frolic?"

NOW!

Take the time to sit down and list five things that you would like to "go outside and play," and then ask your inner-child to join you.

Here's my list:

1. Join a local theater group.
2. Host a karaoke party and sing with your friends.
3. Fill some balloons with water and get soaking wet with your "grandies."
4. Roll down a grassy hill.
5. Go to the seashore and fly a kite.

You're never too old to be a child! Get out there and play!

Affirmation: I make time to play.

NAMASTE

April 5

Resurrection

"Daily, I am reborn through the Christ-consciousness within me."
-Author

The door to yet another delightful spring is swinging open to greet the warbling birds, the burgeoning trees and the vibrant perennial blossoms. It is a transformation not unlike the story of Christ and his resurrection.

Out of the darkness of winter, the flora and fauna once again emerge. Out of the blackness of the crucifixion and the tomb, Christ arose to live, love and teach.

When I contemplate the resurrection, I feel the Christ presence within me. Everyday I can raise myself to a keener sense of spiritual consciousness, thereby experiencing my own personal daily rebirth.

Affirmation: I am reborn each day.

NAMASTE

April 6
Bless All Animals

". . .So out of the ground the Lord God formed every animal of the
field and every bird of the air and brought them to the man
to see what he would call them."
Genesis 2:19

-And they called her Teddi-

This morning, I received an e-mail from a dear friend, telling me that
her dog had made her transition. Teddi was a seventeen-year-old
Pomeranian who looked very much like my little Zen Master, Punkie.
She was a joy to her family and will be missed by them all.

Our precious pets enrich our lives, give us total, unconditional love
and have even been known to lower our blood pressure.

In my home, I have a statue of St. Francis of Assisi, the Patron Saint
of animals and all creation. Every animal has a purpose in the balance
of our ecosystem, as well as being wonderful sources of enjoyment.
Birds give us song, butterflies and lady bugs enrich the earth with color
and squirrels can entertain us for hours.

Enjoy the creatures of the earth—love them.

Dance with the angels, dear Teddi, until we join you on the other
side.

Affirmation: I bless all the animals of the world.

NAMASTE

April 7
Health

"Look to your health; and if you have it praise God, and value it next to a good conscience; for health is the second blessing that we mortals are capable of; a blessing that money cannot buy."
-Izaak Walton

When my granddaughter, who is a nutritionist at Brigham and Women's Hospital in Boston, came home for Christmas this year, I asked if she would help me with my eating choices. (A delicate way to admit I was overweight.)

Over the holidays, I had added to my already fluffy body, more pounds than I needed, and too much sugar was causing havoc to my system.

After she went back to Boston, I phoned her each Monday evening to report my pounds lost, and, she, in turn, sent me menus to ensure that I maintained a balanced diet. She also encouraged me to walk thirty minutes each day.

By following her advice, I have now shed sixteen pounds while my happiness scale has gone up one hundred percent.

When we take care of our bodies through diet, exercise and getting the proper sleep each night, we raise our mood and energy quotients

Add to that a rich spiritual life and there is no limit to our "exuberance barometer."

Affirmation: Today I will start taking care of my body and my soul.

NAMASTE

April 8

Infinite Voice

"Listen carefully to the audible vibrations of God."
-Author

This morning, the Beloved is speaking to me in so many ways.

It is early and through the open windows of my sanctuary, I can hear the chirping and warbling of the birds—my first conversation of the day with Spirit.

I touch the "CD" button on my "magical music box," and the sounds of a gentle waterfall, followed by the tranquil music of an orchestra permeate the room. God always speaks volumes to me through the strings of a violin, the keys of a piano, the ringing of sacred bells, the dulcet tones brought on by the sliding of a bow across the strings of a cello or the slow beating of a drum.

I often lie in bed before sunset and listen—just listen. It is during this time of silent meditation that Intuitive Mind never fails to "pop" words into my head. It is these words that link themselves into sentences and become my book. I love these miraculous moments of co-creation with God.

Take a few minutes today and just listen—listen to the bubbling of a stream, the waves of the ocean, the discernible vibrations of life all around you—the voice of the Beloved.

Affirmation: Today I will hear God everywhere and in everything.

NAMASTE

April 9
Live With Passion

"I know that something exciting and awesomely
wonderful will happen today."
-Author

Above the windows on two walls in my sanctuary, I have placed large wooden letters that read, "I know that something exciting and awesomely wonderful will happen today."

Each morning, I eagerly enter my special room and read that tantalizing affirmation, knowing that the words will come true for me as well as for every sentient being on earth.

I adore living a life of passion, letting each and every day present me with miracles, both expected and unexpected, and the knowing that there is a great adventure ahead. And life never lets me down.

There are exciting hours of writing and the awesomely wonderful times spent with friends and family.

Replenish your soul each morning by repeating my wall affirmation and make it come true for you. Soon you will find yourself living a more passionate, awesome life.

Affirmation: Today I will look for wonderful adventures and serendipitous miracles.

NAMASTE

April 10
Co-Creating

Today, I co-create with the Beloved!
Words like spouting water from a fountain
Spring upward from the Writer-Source within,
As I dance among a constant flow of thoughts
And feelings streaming out onto the pages of my mind.

-Author

It gives me great comfort to know that I do not write alone, that what I say comes from a place deep within. My words are not really my words. In this profession, God becomes "Creative Consciousness," "Infinite Mind," and, sometimes, "All-Knowing Wordsmith."

How does your understanding of Spirit fit into your profession? Is He, perhaps, "The Erudite Teacher," "The Sacred Healer," or, maybe, "The Benevolent Business Partner?"

No matter what our vocations, there is great importance in recognizing that we are not alone in what we do. At any time, we can call on the Omniscient Associate and He will be there for us.

Affirmation: In my profession, I use the mind of God.

NAMASTE

April 11
Attuned to the Seasons

"I am a monarch of all I survey . . . ."
-Henry David Thoreau

In writing this book, I have become more attuned to the rhythmic changes of the seasons.

Today, everywhere I look, the world is dressed for spring. Color emerges from the earth to carpet the hills with vibrant wild flowers. The gardens of the homes around mine are burgeoning patchworks of glorious red geraniums, pink roses and yellow daffodils.

Summer brings with it the lethargic slowing of my life. Days spent mostly indoors out of the smothering heat, more time for meditation, prayer and delicious hours of writing. And then there are the balmy evenings sitting on the front porch with candles lit and faux potted ficus trees hung with small, twinkling lights that mimic those overhead in the sky.

My favorite of all of the seasons is autumn with its juicy red pomegranates, its orange and yellow pumpkins and the glorious coloring of the leaves on my two crepe myrtles and my three camphor trees. Each year my leafy friends attempt to out-dress each other with their radiant garments of red, orange and gold.

The winters of my life are filled with boiling pots of soup, crusty loaves of bread and friends and family gathered around a dining room table of love. Winter is a season of celebrating those nearest and dearest to my heart.

Our lives are like the four seasons: the joy and renewal of spring; the warmth and contemplation of summer; the color and charm of autumn; and the sustenance and love of winter.

Affirmation: I recognize and celebrate each season.

NAMASTE

April 12
Faith

"Mystery on all sides! And faith the only star in this darkness and
uncertainty."
-Henri Amiel

Faith is the foundation of our relationship with the Beloved. It is the
knowing of "not knowing," the complete trust in Infinite Truth apart
from logical evidence.

It is in faith that we open our hearts to God's perfect plan. It is our
faith that dispels fear, reminding us that Spirit is the only presence and
force in our lives.

We read in Hebrews 11:1, "Now faith is the substance of things
hoped for, the evidence of things not seen."

Affirmation: Through faith, I am fearless and free.

NAMASTE

April 13
Letting Go of the Balloon

"Astronomy compels the soul to look upwards and
leads us from this world to another."
-Plato

What happens when you let go of a balloon filled with helium? It wafts upward into the heavens. It can't help it—it just does.

Similarly, what happens when we "let go and let God?" Just like the helium-filled balloon, we ascend to the heights of our full potential—being that which we came on earth to be.

Affirmation: I will let go of the string of ego and ascend to my highest potential.

NAMASTE

April 14
Allow Only Good Thoughts

"The Lord searcheth all hearts and understands all the
imaginations of the thoughts."
I Chronicles 28:9

When our thoughts toward ourselves are tender and kind, the power behind those thoughts carry an impact far greater than we realize.

As we experience adverse conditions in our lives, we can blame ourselves or we can grasp the knowing that God is in us. Infinite Mind is able to take us from negative, accusatory thoughts to being an open channel for the positive.

God is in everything, even our misfortunes and adversities.

Affirmation: Today I allow nothing but good thoughts to come to me and through me.

NAMASTE

April 15

Tea Anyone?

"There are few hours in my life more agreeable than the hour
dedicated to the ceremony known as afternoon tea."
-Henry James

Yesterday, my neighbor and close friend, Linda, invited me to join her
for a day out, a time away from my creative endeavors.

We traveled to Seal Beach, a mere forty-five minutes from our
homes, where we spent the morning hours browsing through the quaint
seaside shops, purchasing small trinkets that simply could not be left
behind.

Around noontime, Linda asked, "How would you like to experience
'all things tea and fairies?'" Being an avid fan of both the refreshing drink
and the impish, winged sprites, I agreed that I would love to.

As we entered the "Fairy Tea Cottage," we also passed into another
world—a world of fairies and teapots. The pixie-like creatures and
colorful tea vessels sat in clusters on an antique lowboy, two antique
china cabinets as well as atop a charming mahogany fireplace. Fairy
paintings hung on every wall.

The tables, artfully covered with gold or cranberry cloths overlaid
with lace table toppers, held red-beaded candle holders encircled by
berries—some frosted and others simply cranberry in color.

Feeling like children at a tea party, Linda and I ordered, not the
"Garden Fairy Tea," nor the "Queen of the Fairies Tea," but the "Twinkle
Tea," which was shown in the menu as being for customers ten-years-
of-age or under.

Loretta Fox, our "Tea Mistress," made an "ordering exception." She
allowed us to be two little ten-year-old girls.

My friend and I chatted while enjoying our peanut butter and
jelly finger sandwiches and miniature scones with whipped cream

and raspberry jam. Our individual pots of tea with matching cups and saucers were beautifully adorned—mine with pink cabbage roses and Linda's with bright blue hyacinths.

For dessert, we each enjoyed a very large, fat sugar cookie iced with luscious pink frosting and topped with multi-colored sprinkles. We daintily ate this yummy treat with a fork, sipping tea between each bite.

Our day ended with blissful memories of "tea for two," and a promise of more future "artists' holidays."

Sharing tea with a close friend is all about being present. With it comes an atmosphere of intimacy—a ceremony known as afternoon tea.

Affirmation: Today I will take bread and water and magically transform it into tea and toast—or, perhaps, I'll join a friend at a nearby tea house.

NAMASTE

April 16
Listen to Your SPS

"In all thy ways acknowledge Him and He shall direct thy paths."
-Proverbs 3:6

While having lunch with my daughter and son-in-law, the subject of Eric's GPS (Global Positioning System) came up. I asked him how it worked because the whole idea of being able to put in an address and then let some voice lead you to your destination seemed totally "woo-woo" to me.

He explained that he enters the address of where he wants to go, and then his GPS unit sends a signal up to a multitude of satellites and when at least four of them recognize where his unit is, it guides him to his destination through a computerized voice speaking to him.

At home, later that evening, I got to thinking that we all have a similar guidance system, one I have chosen to call our "SPS" (Spiritual Positioning System.)

God knows exactly where we are at all times. All we have to do is tell Him where we want to go—state our intention—and then let that path unfold, listening as He directs us to our destination.

Affirmation: As I meditate, I receive Divine Guidance.

NAMASTE

April 17
Conscious Contact

"Closing my eyes and reaching out with my heart,
I contact the Beloved."
-Author

"What if?" Those two small words can bring forth so many answers, and, at the same time, a plethora of questions.

Today, I want to show you God. I want to make that Sacred Entity so real for you that you can literally reach out and touch It. But I can't. You have to make that connection for yourself.

To each of us, God is such a personal, private Being that we can only experience that Presence on an individual basis.

Right now, close your eyes and feel the Beloved.

Affirmation: What if, today, I discover God?

NAMASTE

April 18
Turn Up Your Rheostat

"When we turn up our spiritual rheostat, life just naturally gets brighter."
-Author

We have a built-in rheostat in each of two floor lamps in our dining room. Depending on how much light we want, or don't want, we turn a small knob on the side of the lamps, causing them to become brighter or dimmer.

The electrical power to these lamps is always there, but, with the rheostat, we have the ability to control the current within the circuit.

Spirit is similar to that galvanic power; His presence and energy is always within us. How much we allow that Infinite Light to flow through depends on us.

Affirmation: Today I turn up my spiritual rheostat.

NAMASTE

April 19

The Obstacles of Life

"The obstacle is the path."
-Zen saying

When my former husband died, fear grabbed me like the clutching tentacles of a giant, black octopus. It took me years to realize that his death was a valuable lesson, an assignment on my pathway to enlightenment.

Because I had always been told that I alone controlled my life, my natural reaction to that which I had no power over was fear—HUGE FEAR!

My fear slowly subsided when I realized that "the obstacle is the path." This particular "bump in the road" brought with it the strengthening of me as an individual, and the knowing that I am so much more than, and definitely because of, everything that happens to me.

Affirmation: My "obstacles" are merely my "lessons."

NAMASTE

April 20

The Sacred Raindrops of God

"The thirsty earth soaks up the rain, and drinks, and gapes for drink again."
-Abraham Cowley

Rain pelts to earth in a syncopated rhythm bouncing off sidewalks and trees surrounding my house. Steam, like low-lying fog, races along the street. The musty smell of earth, and breezes fresh with cool cleansing air, permeate the atmosphere—the heralding of spring.

In the garden, the lavender trumpets on the climbing vines prance awkwardly when kissed by the cascading water from the pewter skies. Red roses and purple iris strain upward, drinking in the heavenly liquid.

On my front porch in this late afternoon, an afternoon blessed by a sudden April downpour, there is a monastic feel of resting in a sacred temple. In this holy place, the symphony of God's liquid song lulls me into a deep meditation of thankfulness and peace.

Affirmation: I rejoice in God's damp blessings.

NAMASTE

April 21
Immortality

"He will through life be master of himself and a happy man who from day to day can have said, 'I have lived!'"
-Horace

Unlike the East, we in the West tend to deny death. We don't know how to approach someone who has lost a loved one—"It's just so hard to know what to say," is our mantra.

I wonder, if we lived our lives in the opulent splendor that we were put here to experience, would we then be ready and willing to make our transition when the time comes?

Is God dead? No. So, if God never dies and we are made in His likeness, we, too, will never die. All of the major beliefs concur that death is just another step on our eternal pathway.

I would like you to consider three questions:

1. Are you following your bliss?
2. Is loving and being loved what matters most to you?
3. Is God central in your life?

If your answer is "yes" to all three of these questions, then my belief is that you will close your eyes at life's end and slip quietly and peacefully beyond the veil.

Simplistic? You bet!

Affirmation: My death is a mirror of my life.

NAMASTE

April 22

Happy Earth Day

"We have not inherited the earth from our fathers
We are borrowing it from our children."
-Possible Indian Proverb

Earth day is being celebrated this month. Don't you love that thought? It makes me want to run out and buy a bushel of organic vegetables and fruits to bring my body into nutritional balance. It also challenges me to use the many eco-friendly cleaning products that not only keep our houses fresh and clean, but also our atmosphere.

It is equally important to feed our spiritual bodies during this springtime renewal.

One of the most satisfying ways for me to do this is by enjoying the splendor of nature. Lucky you, if you live in the country! But if you live, as I do, in the "asphalt jungle," you can always visit a nearby nursery and walk among the plants and flowers, stopping to smell the fragrant gardenia or rose and thanking God for His marvelous creations.

Go Green!

Be happy and healthy!

Affirmation: Today I think of ways to go green in order that my children and grandchildren can inherit a cleaner earth.

NAMASTE

April 23
Too Much is Wonderful

"To me, it is a mortal sin not to enjoy all the good things
life has to offer."
-Author

In my kitchen I have a serving tray with words written on it that Mae West was purported to have said. It reads, "Too much of a good thing is wonderful."

I so concur with those words. I don't believe we can ever have enough of the goodness that life has to offer us.

The Jewish Talmud teaches us that, "A person will have to answer for everything that his eye beheld and he did not consume." (Jerusalem Talmud, Kiddushin 4:12.)

We must live each day of our lives enjoying all of the bally-hoo and fanfare we deserve.

It is essential that we think of ourselves as queens, stepping out onto the red carpet of another twenty-four hours, greeted by the blasting trumpets of "Too much of a good thing."

Affirmation: I will accept all of the wonderfulness that life has to offer.

NAMASTE

April 24
Are You a "Nowaholic?"

"Wisely and slow; they stumble that run fast."
-William Shakespeare

I am addicted to "now." When a thought comes that I need to rearrange furniture, I want to do it NOW!

If a new book written by my favorite author is due in at the bookstore Tuesday, I want it TUESDAY!

Somebody needs to concoct a "wait" pill for me.

We live in an age where the keyword is "now." Life is traveling at breakneck speed with instant coffee and instant soup, heated in quick-cooking microwaves. Then there are the fast-food restaurants that have taught us that slowing down is surely a cardinal sin.

We read or watch TV while walking on our treadmills and then order pepperoni pizza delivered to our homes so we don't have to cook or go out to eat. We have instant potatoes, one-minute oatmeal and five-minute rice.

It just might benefit us to slow down and smell the roast cooking in the oven or get off the exercise equipment and take a long walk in nature.

As for the latest book due out on Tuesday? Well, I'll have to think about that one.

Affirmation: Today I will slow down.

NAMASTE

April 25
An Allowing God

"God is in the midst of our discomfort."
-Author

How many of us think when we are in physical or emotional pain that if we just "give it to God" it will instantly be healed and then find it's not. Don't get me wrong, I do believe in miracles, but I have found that the Beloved doesn't always work that way.

We sometimes fake that we're feeling "just fine" so that we don't burden others with our complaints. Or maybe we wonder if we were wrong and there just plain is no God.

When on earth did we decide that God was into quick fixes? Where did we get the notion that He is a "Magical Houdini" instead of the "Infinite Midwife," standing beside us, awaiting the birth of spiritual lessons learned and patience born?

Affirmation: God sometimes allows me growth through pain.

NAMASTE

April 26
The Law of Attraction

"What we expect, that we shall find."
-Plato

How do we manifest what comes into our lives?

When we continually focus on what we don't want, we get what we don't want. When we focus on what we desire and do the work to achieve it, we get positive results.

It's called "The Law of Attraction." Everything in our lives, whether negative or positive, responds to the stories that we tell ourselves over and over. Things like, I'll always be fat because mom was fat; everybody's out to get me; it never fails, I invariably get four colds a year.

If we revise our stories from gloom and doom to positive affirmations, our lives miraculously improve.

Affirmation: I use The Law of Attraction to change my life.

NAMASTE

April 27

Hospitality

"Do not neglect to show hospitality to strangers, for thereby some have entertained angels unawares."
-Hebrews 13:12

It's easy to offer a loving and generous reception to those we know. But what about the strangers we encounter in life? Shouldn't hospitality be part of our essential spiritual practice?

I am not negating the value of teaching our children not to go with strangers that approach them; I'm speaking here of smiling at someone as you pass them by, asking the woman in line next to you at the grocery store how old her adorable child is, or, perhaps, buying a can of peanuts and giving it to a homeless person on the street.

Hospitality is sometimes stepping out of our comfort zone in order to turn an uncaring world around one soul at a time.

Affirmation: My hospitable nature embraces strangers as well as friends.

NAMASTE

April 28

Inspired Through Purpose

"Whatever a poet writes with enthusiasm and a divine
inspiration is very fine."
-Democritus

When you discover the purpose for your life, what you came here to do,
it is the ultimate act of becoming whole.

You spiral upward, transcending anything and everything you've
ever felt and done before.

Patanjali wrote:

When you are inspired by some great purpose,
all your thoughts break their bonds.
Your mind transcends limitation, your consciousness
expands in every direction and you find yourself
in a new, great and wonderful world.
Dormant forces, faculties and talents become alive,
and you discover yourself to be a greater person
by far than you ever dreamed yourself to be.

Affirmation: I discover my purpose and my mind expands.

NAMASTE

April 29

Appreciation

"Gratefulness opens wide our hearts."
-Author

We speak often of our appreciation for art, delicious food, and, perhaps beautiful music. But what about our family and friends? How often do we tell them or show them what a blessing they are to us?

Have you thanked those special people in your life for their love and support, their faithfulness and encouragement?

If not, take time today to send an inspiring card or e-mail. Perhaps you might treat them to lunch or a bouquet of flowers from your garden.

Every act of gratitude opens us to a greater feeling of love, serenity and joy.

Affirmation: Today I will show my appreciation to someone I love.

NAMASTE

April 30

Nature's Gifts

"Contemplate the glory that God is in everything you see. Breathe in the essence of nature, the trees, flowers and grass."
-Gail Manishor, RScP
From Here to Serenity

This afternoon the sky is an azure blue with puffs of whipped cream clouds whose shapes are in constant flux from the light breeze that moves them about.

The bird feeder hanging from our crepe-myrtle tree was replenished this morning and the wild canaries, mocking birds and wrens are enjoying an afternoon snack.

Nature is so very beautiful—so simple in its freedom to just be. I feel a lingering sense of peace here on my porch, an element of harmony with all of nature that casts a magical spell over me. Here, there is an intimacy with nature that sustains and embraces me and I know myself to be truly blessed.

Affirmation: I commune with nature and am at peace.

NAMASTE

May 1

May Day

"On Richmond Hill there lives a lass
More bright than Mayday morn;
Whose charms all other maids' surpass—
A rose without a thorn.
-Leonard MacNally

When I was a child, May Day was widely celebrated. My sister and I would make and decorate brightly colored construction paper baskets, fill them with an assortment of spring flowers (and, I must confess, weeds as well) and leave them on the neighbors' doorsteps.

A few years ago, I attended a lovely May Day event in a local park. The celebration opened with a young girl walking toward us over a small, grassy knoll. She was dressed as the Queen of May in a white, flowing gown. On her head, she wore a wreath of bright flowers intertwined with sprigs of baby's breath and fern.

After a picnic lunch, everyone danced around a May Pole decorated with long strands of multicolored, crepe paper ribbon. When the music started, we each took a strand of the colorful ribbon in our hand and laughed and sang together while going round and round the pole.

Today, why not join your children in celebrating May Day. Fabricate colorful baskets, fill them with flowers, or maybe even candy, and deliver them to your neighbors, to Grandma, or to yourself.

Affirmation: I will enjoy a May Day celebration.

NAMASTE

May 2
World Laughter Day

"My best days are the days when I laugh the loudest."
-Author

World Laughter Day is usually celebrated on the first Sunday of May. It is a day when the world comes together to laugh—to spread happiness and joy throughout the world.

The Laughter Club is a global movement, uniting mankind through unconditional love and a few good chuckles. It is a non-religious, non-racial and non-profit organization committed to generating good health, joy and world peace through laughter.

It has been said that, on average, children laugh up to 300 times a day, adults, only 15 times in a day.

Laughing works the muscles of our face, chest and abdomen and a hearty guffaw stimulates the heart rate, causes us to breathe deeply and releases endorphins—the happiness hormones.

When we giggle and chortle, we release the joy of our souls out into the universe.

Affirmation: Today I will find reason to laugh.

NAMASTE

May 3

How Important is a Smile?

"But a genuine smile really gives us a feeling of freshness . . ."
-The Dalai Lama
In My Own Words

I love smiles!

My little Zen Master, Punkie, wags her tail when my son comes to visit, and then she rolls over and smiles a wide, ingratiating grin. On occasion, she has been known to smile at the rest of us, but it's for Michael that she beams the brightest.

Every time I see a statue of the Laughing Buddha, it makes me want to grin right back. How joyful Buddha must feel, I think to myself. And, then, I strive to keep happiness in my own life—happy thoughts, happy people, happy experiences.

In his book, *In My Own Words*, the Dalai Lama writes, "The more we care for the happiness of others, the greater our own sense of well-being becomes . . . ."

Smile at everyone you meet and watch your own happiness increase.

Affirmation: Today I will smile, and, as I do, my inner joy will expand.

NAMASTE

May 4

Expect Delays

"The joys of life often include 'Plan B.'"
-Author

We were off on another wondrous adventure, my friend, Linda and I, when, without warning, we were forced to take "Plan B, then C, and, alas, D."

Together, we had carefully mapped out a well-organized schedule. Our intent was to visit a famous landmark in a nearby town—a more than century-old, completely furnished Victorian home. After that we would go to the lovely Mission Inn for lunch followed by a browse through the many interesting shops surrounding the Inn.

And then what happened?

Life—that succession of unpredicted events that seem to appear out of nowhere!

Just before starting on our venture, Linda read in the paper that there was an antique car show scheduled that would make it impossible for us to get anywhere near the Mission Inn.

So, putting our beautiful, feminine heads together, we revised our plans and drove toward the freeway that would take us to our destination. The on-ramp, however, was closed due to an accident.

Okay. No problem. We'll simply drive to the next on-ramp.

HA!

We were halted by a Cinco de Mayo parade, marching through the center of our small town.

Turning her van around, Linda routed us to yet another on-ramp and we heaved a mutual sigh of relief as we finally entered the freeway, only to be deluged by at least two hundred motorcyclists out for a Saturday afternoon ride. We raced to the nearest off ramp, deciding that the side streets might better keep us out of harm's way.

Linda and I burst into laughter when a flatbed truck passed us. The enormous sign it was carrying read, "EXPECT DELAYS."

In spite of all our unplanned hindrances, the day was perfect! We had a delightful tour through the Victorian home and then journeyed across town where we enjoyed a delicious lunch in an outdoor garden setting and wandered through fascinating shops that I never knew existed.

Call it fate, serendipity or destiny, our day was a great success and the Mission Inn still dances in our minds for a future outing.

Affirmation: I joyously and gracefully accept the Plan "B's" of life.

NAMASTE

May 5
Hope

"Hope is the thing with feathers
That perches in the soul
And sings the tunes without the words
And never stops at all."
-Emily Dickinson

Hope is desire, something within us that leaves us open to a promising future, a passion for the amazing miracles that have yet to be revealed.

Hope is also an attitude, one that we can cultivate over time by letting go of our negativity and envisioning only our highest good.

By staying optimistic, we can become a contagious force of hope for ourselves and for those around us.

Affirmation: Today, and every day, I will let hope perch in my soul.

NAMASTE

May 6

What Questions Would You Like to Ask God?

"For every question there is an answer."
-Author

We all wish at times that we could confront God with the many unanswered questions that come up for us. Questions such as; Why must we experience natural disasters? Why do people suffer poverty and hunger? Or, maybe, why did you take my loved one at such a young age?

The Beloved invites us to ask these questions and He will respond. All we have to do is wait and listen.

Sit with any question that you might have at various times during the day. Do this for as long as it takes.

When my husband died at the age of fifty-seven, I not only asked, "Why?" I screamed it out at the top of my lungs! I was hurt, angry, lost and yet the answer came. One day I heard the Beloved say, "It was his time to go and it is your time to go on." It has been twenty-seven years since I heard that answer, and for the last twenty-five years, I have been happily remarried to another wonderful, loving man.

Our answers may not come immediately, they may not be what we want to hear, and, sometimes, we may not receive an answer at all for a few years. Or, perhaps a book might slide off of a shelf that contains the answer. Just keep asking and listening.

Affirmation: I will ask my questions and then listen to that Still, Small Voice within.

NAMASTE

May 7
The Wolves Within

"The wolf also shall dwell with the lamb . . ."
Isaiah 11:6

Here we are again on my front porch, where I would like to share with you a Cherokee legend entitled, The Wolves Within.

"An old Grandfather said to his grandson who came to him with anger at a friend who had done him an injustice, 'Let me tell you a story.

'I too, at times, have felt a great hate for those that have taken so much, with no sorrow for what they do.

'But hate wears you down, and does not hurt your enemy. It is like taking poison and wishing your enemy would die. I have struggled with these feelings many times. It is as if there are two wolves inside me. One is good and does no harm. He lives in harmony with all around him and does not take offense when no offense was intended. He will fight only when it is right to do so, and in the right way.

'But the other wolf, ah! He is full of anger. The littlest thing will set him into a fit of temper. He fights everyone, all the time, for no reason. He cannot think, because his anger and hate are so great. It is helpless anger, for his anger will change nothing.

'Sometimes, it is hard to live with these two wolves inside me, for both of them try to dominate my spirit.'

The boy looked intently into his Grandfather's eyes and asked, 'Which one wins, Grandfather?'

The Grandfather smiled and quietly said, 'The one I feed.'"

Affirmation: Today, I will feed the harmonious wolf within.

NAMASTE

May 8
A Quiet Walk

"Hear the voice of the Bard!
Who present, past and future sees,
Whose ears have heard
The Holy Word
That walk'd among the ancient trees.
-William Blake

Meditation is a wonderful way to quiet your mind. Another method to stop all that useless prattle in your head is to walk—walk until your "monkey mind" ceases its endless chatter.

Find a route, if you can, that includes plenty of nature. Amongst the trees, bushes and flowers, you will discover that being in this God-created atmosphere can help you change your outlook. Problems will become insignificant in comparison to the durable beauty and strength of an old tree, the gentle swaying of a colorful, long-stemmed delphinium or the sweet smell of a honeysuckle vine in full bloom.

Walking leads to clarity and peace. The mind naturally opens to itself as your feet stroll in rhythm to that of the Great Cosmic Creator.

Affirmation: In nature I will find peace.

NAMASTE

May 9

Zen Meditation

"I leave the dark side of the moon and merge into
The Oneness of the Now."
-Nancy Nisonger

"It is time to clear your mind, go into the silence.

"Take several deep breaths, quieting the chatter within, then step upward into space, drift on a cloud, swing on a star, or, perhaps, you'll want to spread your wings and fly.

"You feel yourself skipping throughout eternity on a spiritual high, doing floating somersaults in space. In this mist, you surrender and let go of all that does not serve a meaningful purpose. You are one with the Universe. You are one with Soul. Here you feel the pureness, the presence of Spirit. You are everywhere, yet you are nowhere. You are one with The All.

"These Zen moments in time are yours just for the asking."
-Nancy Nisonger
From her class
Stepping Into Soul

Affirmation: Today I will practice Zen Meditation.

NAMASTE

May 10
Flying With the Great Winged Spirit

"My thoughts, like a great blue heron, soar with Infinite Mind."
-Author

Outside my living room window, this morning, a great blue heron rises from the pond after his first meal of the day. He glides majestically back and forth, seemingly without purpose.

I have been sitting here, pen in hand, for over an hour, staring out the window. My mind, like the drifting heron, glides aimlessly, seeking for words, food for thought, to fill the blank page before me.

Then, slowly, a revelation emerges from deep within. Finishing this book is not what is important. It is my relationship, my flight, with the Beloved that is the essence, the essential component in my writing.

Affirmation: It is not that I fly but Who soars with me that counts.

NAMASTE

May 11
Enlightening Books

"Nature and books belong to the eyes that see them."
-Ralph Waldo Emerson

Yesterday someone gifted me with two new books, a copy of the Tao Te Ching, a new English Version with foreword and notes by Stephen Mitchell, and the companion book, A Thousand Names For Joy, by Byron Katie with Stephen Mitchell. These two books, read together, contain powerful messages from the great Tao.

How precious my spiritual books are to me. Over many years, I have collected hundreds of them.

I do believe that if I ever go into an assisted-living compound, my room will have to be as large as the Library of Congress, with as many shelves.

My precious books are like the bread crumbs in the Hansel and Gretel fairy tale. They have led me toward great spiritual growth along my pathway to enlightenment.

Affirmation: I thank God for my library.

NAMASTE

May 12
Opening the Gifts of Our Soul

"There is no painful effort, but it is the spontaneous
flowing of the thought.
Shakespeare made his Hamlet as a bird weaves its nest."
-Ralph Waldo Emerson

In his book, *Soul at Home*, David Milligan writes, "I often get compliments on a lovely painting that hangs in my office. My mother was the artist and it was her only painting. She bought oil paints one summer, took a postcard of Huntington Lake in California and painted a beautiful depiction of the scene. She spent the next 30-odd years of her life saying, 'I wish I had the time to paint again.' After her retirement, Mom went out and bought new paints and all the accompanying supplies. Yet, in over ten years of retirement, she never found the time to paint."

Today, as we gather on my front porch, I want us to think about what our special gifts are and how they might be lying dormant, waiting to be used. I have prepared a symbolic basket of presents—one for each of you. All of the boxes are embellished with a distinct flower—a bright yellow jonquil, a soft pink rose, or, perhaps, a velvety purple orchid.

I want you to carefully choose the box whose flower speaks to your Elizabeth Barrett Browning heart or, perhaps, your Picasso soul—one that touches you very personally.

The Beloved gave each of us a special gift—and, sometimes, multiple gifts, which we are to use, both to bless ourselves and others. (Normally, it's something that we dearly love to do.) There is the gift of teaching, of writing, of singing or speaking. Then, there are others as well, such as sewing, cooking, quilting, crocheting or painting. I could go on forever naming those things that Infinite Love brought us here on earth to express.

Gaze at your flower for a time and then close your eyes and let Source speak to you—tell you what your special gift is and how you might use it. Or, perhaps, thank Him for those gifts that you already use everyday.

Now let's open our presents together and discover another offering, one that God gave to all of us.

Go ahead, open your gift.

The silver heart-shaped pendant contained within the box symbolizes the gift of love. We all have it, we all can share it and we all definitely require it.

Affirmation: Using my special gifts fills my life with joy.

NAMASTE

May 13
A Bamboo Love Affair

"The rustling of leaves,
The clacking of hollow, wooden stems swaying in the breeze,
God's bamboo concerto of love."
-Author

Yesterday I had an affair—A love affair with hundreds of tall, willowy bamboos.

These handsome Romeos encircle, encapsulate and dance around the home of two friends.

Theo and Doreen invited Bill and me to visit them and, together, "watch the bamboo grow." Now, I've heard of "watching the grass grow," but, bamboo?

An hour before we arrived, Theo measured a couple of the new baby shoots. Sure enough, when we went out to investigate the markings, they had grown half of an inch. Theo informed us that bamboos are capable of growing up to twenty-four inches or more a day, over a period of three to four months during their growth spurt.

As we watched the incredible shoots, the mothers of these sprouts, along with hundreds of other bamboo family members, swayed an encouraging dance of growth around and about these new babies.

I stood in the midst of this woody cathedral, listening to the symphony of rustling leaves and the syncopated clacking of thick stems, and yearned for a baton—longed to be the conductor of these rhythmic objects of my love.

A Malaysian legend tells of a man who, while sleeping under a bamboo plant, dreams of a beautiful woman; he wakes up and breaks the bamboo stem, discovering the woman inside.

Yesterday, I was that woman.

Affirmation: Today I will have a love affair with nature.

NAMASTE

May 14

Looking at the World Through the Eyes of Our Souls

"The mass of men lead lives of quiet desperation."
-Henry David Thoreau

We often look to our external world to get all of our needs met; but once we have that expensive mansion, the shiny new sports car, or even the latest technological gadget, we still feel incomplete.

In this incompleteness, we need to look at life through the eyes of our souls.

We are so much more than our physical accoutrements.

Our essential possessions are our healthy bodies, the nature that surrounds us and the knowledge that we have a Higher Power with whom we can co-create an entire life.

Affirmation: Today, I look at the world through the eyes of my soul.

NAMASTE

May 15

Joy

".... and he [Jesus] said unto them: Blessed are ye because of your faith. And now behold, my joy is full."

3 Nephi 17:20

The Book of Mormon

The verse above shows that Jesus was filled with joy because of the faith shown to him by his followers. And, before that, in verse 17, his followers express what joy they felt when they heard him "pray for us unto the Father."

Joy is an emotion of love that was expressed in the days of Christ, and that can be expressed over and over in our lives today.

Julian of Norwich, a fourteenth-century English mystic wrote, "The fullness of joy is to behold God in everything."

Joy is evident wherever we look. It sparkles through every star in the midnight sky. It dances with each fluttering autumn leaf. It wafts on the air through the fragrance of spring flowers.

When we allow the Christ-consciousness within to fill us with joy, we give ourselves permission to celebrate God in everything and everyone around us.

Affirmation: Today I will express my joy.

NAMASTE

May 16
Challenge Yourself

"I know of no more encouraging fact than the unquestionable ability of man to elevate his life by a conscious endeavor."
-Henry David Thoreau

We all need relevant challenges in order to make our lives more inspiring, more interesting. I'm not speaking here of the disrupting occurrences that sometimes plague us. I'm talking about the stimulating activities that stretch our minds, get our blood pumping, and stir our imaginations

For me, it is the challenge of "wordsmithing," hammering out those just-right phrases and sentences. For my husband, Bill, who spends hours at his scroll saw, it is the urgent bidding to take an ordinary piece of fine wood and transform it into a delicate, lace pattern. In the end, both of us are simply enjoying the challenge of inspired creativity.

What challenges you? What is missing in your life that, perhaps, once kindled a fire within you whenever you even thought about it?

Get to it! Challenge yourself!

Affirmation: Today I accept the challenge!

NAMASTE

May 17

Duality

"The dark and the light—a duality belonging to all of us."
-Author

Have you ever wondered how you can feel so very loving toward someone one minute and the next, in a spurt of anger, you want to throw something at him?

It's called "duality." And it's something we all possess.

When I first discovered how angry I could feel, it frightened me so, I found myself shaking. How could I, who wrote of love, feel this way? Well, I'll tell you, it knocked the self-righteousness part of me on its keester—sent me reeling.

Possessing both the light and the dark sides merely make us whole. It humbles us.

Affirmation: Through my dark side, I recognize the unconditional love of God."

NAMASTE

May 18

God is Everywhere and in Everything

"When we swim with the dolphins, we swim with God.
When we ride on the back of a horse, God carries us.
The Infinite Creator abides in everything and in every creature."
-Author

I often forget that my plea for God to show Herself to me, give me some physical evidence of Her existence, is something She does everyday and every night.

This morning I got a call from my twelve-year-old grandson. His excitement crackled through the telephone when he said, "Guess what just happened to me? I was standing at the dining room window, looking out on the patio at the planter, when a hummingbird stopped sucking on a red flower and flew over to the window. Honest! He looked straight at me, like—forever!!"

Chanse knew that, through this tiny bird, he was mind-talking with God, having a soul-to-soul communication with Everything That Is.

The Beloved has so many ways of showing Herself to us—the rising and setting of the sun each day, the budding of leaves on the trees each spring, even the bulb that knows instinctively it is an iris, pushing through the earth in all its purple splendor.

How can we watch the constant ebb and flow of the ocean waves or the cycle of the moon and not understand that there exists a Mighty Creative Force—a Loving Existence that some call God?

Affirmation: The proof of God's existence is everywhere.

NAMASTE

May 19

Being Sensitive Toward Others

"Speak the truth, but speak it palatably."
-Sanskrit Proverb

It is always best to be truthful with others, but, oh my, how difficult that can sometimes be.

Maybe a good idea would be to, first, put yourself in the other person's shoes. This will make it easier to speak with empathy and let go of judgment. Confucius called it "candor with consideration."

Truthfulness is good. But it is equally important that our honesty be used with care. We must remember to use words that are both sensitive and respectful.

Affirmation: I am both honest and sensitive.

NAMASTE

May 20
We Are All Powerful, Intelligent and Capable

"We interact with people from the platform of our own self-esteem."
-Author

How many times have we allowed ourselves to be a pawn on the chessboard of life? We give others permission to play us from their own needs, beliefs and discretions.

Often, because of negative messages received in childhood, we become masters of illusion. We pretend we don't know what is good for us or what might be right decisions for our lives. Everyone else seems more intimidatingly intelligent, more capable, and, thus, better able to make our decisions for us.

NOT!!!

Step outside the curtain of illusion. Take your pawn-self out of the chess game. Admit the truth and embrace the fact that you are made in the image of God, that you are intelligent, capable and able to do your own decision-making. Then watch your life unfold in ways you never thought possible.

Affirmation: Today I accept my own perfect intelligence and capability.

NAMASTE

May 21

Curiosity

"Do cats eat bats? . . . Do bats eat cats? . . . Curiouser and curiouser!"
-Lewis Carroll
Alice In Wonderland

It is important, I think, to question why we are here and what it means to be here.

When I look into the face of a newborn, I ask myself, "What is the meaning of this new life? Why is she here? What is he here to do?"

The stars in the heavens, the earth on which we walk, the very body that carries us from place to place, these things constantly amaze me and, at the same time, arouse my curiosity.

Ralph Waldo Emerson said, "Undoubtedly we have no questions to ask which are unanswerable. We must trust the perfection of the creation so far, as to believe that whatever curiosity the order of things has awakened in our minds, the order of things can satisfy.

Affirmation: I will never lose my curiosity about why I exist and what my existence means.

NAMASTE

May 22
Ode to Enough

"Enough is as good as a feast."
-John Heywood

I have not laughed enough.
I have not loved enough.
I have not danced enough.
I have not sung enough.
I have not cried enough.
Today I will start and that will be enough.
-Author

Affirmation: I still have time for enough.

NAMASTE

May 23

We Each Contain All the Colors of the Rainbow

"The soul is dyed the color of its thoughts."
-Marcus Aurelius

Eastern philosophy teaches us that everyone is a walking rainbow. We have within us seven energy centers or "chakras." These chakras range from the lower center of red and orange, up to the solar plexus of yellow, the green heart chakra, blue for the throat chakra, indigo for the third eye and violet for the crown chakra at the top of the head.

Children often pick crayons that show how they feel about themselves—pastel colors convey happiness and contentment, bright colors denote strong feeling and black or dark blue can mean sadness or pain.

We often choose our clothes for the day based on the energy of our chakras at the time. Also, we can pick out clothes for the energy that we wish to create. We might pick red or orange for power, yellow for intellect, green for calmness, and pale blue or violet for creativity and peaceful feelings.

Watch the colors that you pick and connect that with how you feel or how you want to feel.

Affirmation: I can be any color of the rainbow.

NAMASTE

Unity

"Behold, how good and how pleasant it is for brethren to
dwell together in unity."
Psalm 133:1

How inspiring it is to hear an orchestra in a blend of different instruments, all performing one great symphony. We get the same high when working together for a common cause.

When unity is broken because of ethnic and political warfare and superficial difference, we become emotionally starved—hungry for the pleasantness and peace of the Infinite One.

Baha'u'llah, the founder of Baha'ism wrote: "O contending peoples and kindreds of the earth! Set your faces toward unity, and let the radiance of its light shine upon you. Gather ye together, and for the sake of God resolve to root out whatever is the source of contention among you."

God wants us to live in unity, neighbors with neighbors, faiths with other faiths, and nations with nations.

Affirmation: I will live in unity.

NAMASTE

May 25
We are All Above Average

"God sees nothing average."
-Author unknown

Once we realize that we are each a unique, one-of-a-kind being, we move ourselves from an "average" status to that of "extraordinary."

You and I are an expression of the One. We came into this world with special gifts and insights. Somewhere along the line as we were growing up, however, someone made us feel "less than," causing confusion, guilt and shame to creep into our perfect selves, giving us low self-esteem.

We are, each one, very special. We possess all of the love and divinity that we inherited from our Father/Mother God. Once you realize and accept this, your life will change forever. There is nothing you cannot accomplish.

Affirmation: I am nothing, if not extraordinary.

NAMASTE

May 26
Go Within and Find Your Soul

"Inside each one of us dwells the answers to all the great questions."
-Author

I am an expression of the Divine Energy and so are you!

Below is a beautiful Hindu legend that tells us where we can go to find this Divine Energy.

"Long ago all men were divine, but mankind so abused the privilege that Brahma, the god of all gods, decided the godhead should be taken away from them. But he had to hide it where man would never find it again. 'Let us bury it deep in the earth,' suggested one god. Brahma said, 'No, man will dig down until he finds it.' 'Then let us throw it into the deepest part of the biggest ocean,' proposed another god. 'Man will learn to dive and someday come across it,' insisted Brahma. 'Then it can be hidden in the clouds atop the highest mountain of the Himalayas.' 'Man will manage to climb that high some day,' Brahma pointed out. 'I have a better idea. Let us hide it where he will never think to look: inside himself.'"

Affirmation: I will look inside and find God.

NAMASTE

May 27

Awesome, Dude!

"Awe is the finest portion of mankind . . . . In awe one feels
profoundly the immense."
-Goethe

What makes you want to scream "Awesome!?"

Is it a blindingly beautiful sunset? A wild ride at Disneyland? Or,
perhaps, it is a room in your house newly decorated and arranged to
make it entirely "your own."

Awe is the ultimate expression of wonder. It causes us to be
profoundly awake and cognizant of the feelings that spark within us.

When we are alone, awe can quietly flow through us as we stand
silent and still, riveted in its embrace.

In awe, we can truly and profoundly feel the Immense.

Affirmation: I am often awestruck by the beauty and excitement around
me.

NAMASTE

May 28

Life is a Spiritual Experience

"Seeing the spiritual in everything gives us a daily
masterpiece of beauty."
-Author

Life is most definitely a spiritual experience, an adventure, a daily proof
that there truly is a Sacred Presence.

As my husband and I drove up to the mountain town of Idyllwild
the other day, we passed by pleated hills, lime green with the leaves
of cottonwood trees resting against the cloud-misted mountains—an
untouched, pristine vista that literally took my breath away.

All we have to do to encounter a spiritual experience is look around
us, open our eyes to the presence of this marvelous universe and view
the gifts of God.

Below is a Native American Prayer that says so well and so simply
how we can experience the sacredness of all life:
"The world before me is restored in beauty.
The world behind me is restored in beauty.
The world below me is restored in beauty.
The world above me is restored in beauty.
All things around me are restored in beauty.
It is finished in beauty."

Affirmation: Today I will experience God in all the beauty around me.

NAMASTE

We are the Hands and Feet of God

"The Divine has no body now on earth but yours, no hands but yours."
-Teresa of Avila

In the Koran, it is written about Allah that, "I was a hidden treasure and I wanted to be known; that is why I created the world."

Allah lets Himself be known through every creation that exists. All we have to do is sit outside and we find ourselves being nurtured by nature, a nature that is Allah wanting to be known.

We, too, are the hands and feet of Allah, another expression of Infinite Creator showing Himself to the world.

Those who understand their innate divinity, understand the sacred nature of creativity and why they are here.

The sixteenth century Spanish saint, Teresa of Avila, said it so perfectly when she wrote:

> The Divine has no body now on earth but yours,
> No hands but yours,
> No feet but yours,
> Yours are the eyes through which to look out
> The Divine's compassion to the world;
> Yours are the feet with which
> The Divine is to go about doing good;
> Yours are the hands with which
> The Divine is to bless all beings now."

Affirmation: I am the hands and feet of God.

NAMASTE

May 30
The Swirling Fog

"The Swirling Fog of Life waltzes me about in a
graceful dance of sacred love."
-Author

Fog dances in misty swirls on the sidewalk beside my house this morning. It hovers, suspended near the surface of the pavement in damp, pirouetting motion.

I fantasize myself becoming very small and jumping into the moist eddy. I allow it to whirl me around and around, turning me this way and that, its essential essence filling and surrounding me.

This misty, swirling fog is a perfect metaphor for God. When I permit the Beloved to take me wherever I need to go, whether through aching distress or ecstatic joy, to penetrate me so completely with the essence of His circulating love, I can then let go and allow the spinning eddy of life to take me full circle.

Affirmation: I let the Swirling Fog of Life guide me.

NAMASTE

May 31
Love Versus War

"Weapons are the tools of violence;
All decent men detest them
Therefore, followers of the Tao never use them."
Interpretation of the Tao Te Ching
Wayne Dyer
Change Your Thoughts—Change Your Life

This month, we celebrate Memorial Day. In doing so, we honor those men and women who gave up their lives for what they believed in—to keep our nation free.

During the Korean conflict in the early fifties, my Navy husband was on-board a ship in the Yellow Sea off the coast of Inchon, Korea.

The ship and its crew were preparing to haul whole refugee villages from North Korea to South Korea. These North Korean people no longer wanted to be under communist rule.

Early one morning, while lying in his bunk, Bill felt heavy with the thought of uprooting these people and their livestock from their generational homes and years of tradition all because of men's useless egos.

Needing to release the pain that he was experiencing, he sat up on the side of his bunk and wrote this heartfelt poem:

"O Lord, on this new year today begun,
Cast on our troubled world a cloak of peace.
Let man's small differences and hates be done,
And all his petty, senseless warrings cease."
-William Dillon

How many wars at the cost of thousands of lives must we endure before we all "get it" that hate and ambivalence must be replaced with love and compassion? When will people finally realize that, in spite of color, creed or sexual preference, we are all soul-connected—all created perfectly by the very same power that brought into existence this vast universe of ours?

Affirmation: Today, and every day, I choose to love.

NAMASTE

June 1

Simplify

"Our life is frittered away with detail . . . Simplify, Simplify."
-Henry David Thoreau

Rudyard Kipling wrote, "Teach us to delight in simple things."

Isn't it the simple things that bring us the most joy? A soothing cup of tea; a sweet, chocolate truffle; an interesting, spell-binding novel; listening to the Gregorian chants sung by the Benedictine monks—these are some of the comforting ways that can help us when we find ourselves fragmented by the busyness of our everyday lives.

Like we do to our rose bushes in January, we need to prune our lives down in order to bloom with the colorful buds of sweet simplicity.

Are you hungry for the luscious satisfaction of uncluttering your life? Let go of one small thing that feels dispensable and indulge in an hour of pure, simple enjoyment.

The Buddha said, "Greater happiness comes with simplicity than with complexity."

Affirmation: I will simplify my life

NAMASTE

June 2

Strengthening Our Bodies and Our Souls

"Your human self is the living temple of your Divine Self. Doesn't your
Divine Self deserve its temple to be as strong
and balanced as possible?"
-Andrew Harvey
The Hope

Through the Divine Feminine, we learn how to mother ourselves, how
to take care of our bodies and our souls. We do this by practicing our
own form of spirituality, by eating a healthy diet and by exercising and
getting enough sleep. These practices allow us to renew ourselves and
live in balance.

In his book, *The Hope,* Andrew Harvey shares the following
beautiful prayer:

"Divine Mother, give me Your eyes so I can see myself through
them and see how holy in Your eyes is my soul, and how holy
in Your eyes is my mind, and how holy in Your eyes is my heart,
and how holy and sacred in Your eyes is my body. Help me be as
merciful and generous with myself as You would always want me
to be; help me honor myself as I have found to my amazement You
honor me; help me live and work from the peace and balance and
compassion from which You live and work and help. Help me in
these ways, Mother, so I can at last truly become the instrument you
need me to become, the sacred instrument of Your compassion in
action that You created me to be, and that I already am in Your holy
and illumined eyes."

Affirmation: Through the Divine Feminine, I will understand how to mother myself.

NAMASTE

June 3
Nuggets of Gold

"Poetic Justice, with her lifted scale,
Where, in nice balance, truth with gold she weighs . . ."
-Alexander Pope

In our lifetime, all that we have manifested is the direct result of our past experiences.

Our current reality is made up of both what we might distinguish as "good" or "bad" moments.

If we dig back into the gold mines of our lives, we can unearth precious nuggets of both the positive and the negative—a less-than-loving parent who taught us how important it is to love our own children, the advice of a dear friend that turned our lives around, or the teacher that made us want to scream each time she corrected our grammar, yet, in her constant correcting, we achieved the writing of a published novel.

These experiences are life's bits of precious ore that can afford us innumerable golden opportunities.

Affirmation: I will see every experience in life as a golden nugget.

NAMASTE

June 4

When Was the Last Time You Heard From Yourself?

"You may depend on it, that poor fellow who walks away with the greatest number of letters, proud of his extensive correspondence, has not heard from himself this long while."
-Henry David Thoreau

Where do we go for our information? Usually it's outside ourselves—our teachers, our gurus, those great masters. And sometimes it is to the post office.

In looking for all of life's answers, what we need to do is stay quiet for a time and listen to that Inward Voice. Quit interrupting the Beloved and just listen.

Our answers come if we will but "be still."

Mr. Thoreau also wrote, "In proportion as our inward life fails, we go constantly and desperately to the post office."

Affirmation: I will go to the post office for stamps and to my sanctuary for messages.

NAMASTE

June 5
Kindness

"Kindness only takes a minute, but that single minute can change an entire life."
-Author

I often bring a cup of tea with me when I settle into my swinging loveseat on the front porch. It's my favorite green tea that has a wise saying on the tag. I don't let myself read the small verse until Punkie and I have settled down with our books and a dog treat. (The books are for me, the treat for her—although I'm quite certain she'd be willing to share.)

This morning the saying at the end of my teabag reads: "Act selfless. You will be infinite." That verse made me think of a young man I met outside of a grocery store a couple of weeks ago. He was a handsome fourteen-year-old who walked up to me asking for a dollar so that he could buy some food.

I offered to buy him groceries and asked what he wanted and why he did not have food at home. He looked down for a moment, scuffed his foot against the sidewalk and replied, "My dad is out of work and we sorta' live on the street."

His buddy, who was with him, said, "He stands in front of the store each afternoon and asks for food, otherwise he wouldn't have any." I found out what school this young man and his friend attended and that the school gave him a free lunch each day.

In further conversation, I discovered that his mother lived out-of-state, that his dad had custody of him and that his father told him he could visit his mother if he got good grades.

Bill and I purchased two bags of groceries and took them out to him. He grinned a thank you, saying, "There's even a whole box of cookies in here!"

I am so proud of this precious boy's ingenuity. He is keeping himself alive any way he can and often, I imagine, at the risk of great rejection.

It doesn't take but a minute to be kind to someone and, in so doing, the rewards you heap upon yourself far outweigh the kindness you extend.

Robert Louis Stevenson said it beautifully when he wrote:

"It is the history of our kindness that alone makes the world tolerable. If it were not for that, for the effect of kind words, kind looks, kind letters . . . I should be inclined to think our life a practical jest in the worst possible spirit."

Affirmation: I will recognize ways to express my Divinity through kind acts

NAMASTE

June 6

The Holy Fountain

"Thou of Life the Fountain art;
Freely let me take of Thee;
Spring Thou up within my heart,
Rise to all eternity."
-Charles Wesley

The Spiritual Center where my husband and I attend each Sunday is situated in a park-like area of our small town. The Center itself is a one-hundred-year-old house surrounded by oak, pine, cedar and pepper trees. The energy in this sacred place is one of peace and overwhelming love—love that flows to and through those who attend.

Outside the dining room, through three large windows, you can see a small pond that is the abode of gold and orange koi and colorful water lilies. Next to this small lagoon sits a stone fountain with the figure of an angel pouring water into the fishpond.

Our center's writing group meets once a month around a large table in this dining room. Viktor, the poet among us, wrote a lovely poem about the fountain. With his permission, I would like to share it with you today.

The Holy Fountain

A fountain stands in a verdant garden
Beside a pond of water most serene,
Nourished from a deep, spring eternal,
Giving freely of its pure goodness to all.

A fountain of stone, tiers three,
Calling forth a visage of the Blessed Trinity.
Spraying, splashing ripples of crystal
Journeying on to an endless eternity.

A fountain sheltered by Cedars, tall,
Majestic, standing protective guardians,
The life-giving, blessed waters
Manifesting strength as the loving hand of God.

A fountain creating a liquid abode
Tranquil lilies of lavender, yellow and green,
Golden, swimming fish, a soaring hawk, red dragonflies, three,
As the first day of creation.

A fountain, one of many sisters
Sharing kindly the waters of Divinity,
Be one Buddhist, Jew or Unbeliever,
Flowing as the abundant Grace of God.

Oh, God, Source of all the waters,
May I be a living fountain,
Dispensing your love, blessings and
Kindness to all arid humanity."
                                    -Viktor Wise

Thank you, Viktor.

Affirmation: Today I will be a living fountain of love.

NAMASTE

June 7
Let the Great Winds Carry You

"Sometimes I go about in pity for myself, and all the while a
great wind is bearing me across the sky."
-Ojibwa saying

The phone rings, I'm in the middle of writing and I know if I lose my
train of thought, I might very well not be able to get it back. I answer
the phone anyway and my grandson is on the other end eager to tell
me about his day. When I hang up, something he said is better than
my original thought and I run to write it down—a great wind bears me
across the sky.

My usual morning meditation time and studying from my spiritual
books is put on hold because I got up late and have only a few minutes
to get ready to meet my family at the local park for a scheduled Saturday
picnic. While the festivities are in full swing, I find myself alone, taking
a meditative walk out in the open air among the trees. Then, while
eating our picnic lunch, my daughter tells me about a wonderful, new
book that would go along with exactly what I've been studying—a
great wind bears me across the sky.

If we allow ourselves to relax into our everyday lives, we can release
our "pity parties" and be swept along by the great winds.

Affirmation: I will quit feeling sorry for myself when life interrupts and
just let the great winds carry me.

NAMASTE

June 8

The Backbone of Creativity

"I am certain of nothing but the holiness of the heart's
affections and the truth of imagination."
-John Keats

With our imaginations, we are able to reach the heights of the impossible. Every great invention, every book, and every lovely painting started in the mind of imagination.

My favorite toy as a child was the graceful flower of a hollyhock plant. I would take my mother's pearl-topped hat pins, pierce them through the top of the bloom to make a head, and dance my "dolls" around the lawn as though they were elegant ballerinas.

Henry Ward Beecher wrote, "Imagination is the secret marrow of civilization, it is the very eye of faith."

Imagination is, indeed, the backbone of all creativity.

Affirmation: I release my mind to wild imagination.

NAMASTE

June 9
Soaring Through Life

"I shall use my time."
-Jack London

You have just so many years to live. What are you doing with those years?
Are you living a brilliantly stimulating life or one of stifling desperation?
Recently, I read an uplifting poem by Jack London—listen and heed:

I would rather be ashes than dust!
I would rather that my spark should
burn out in a brilliant blaze than
it should be stifled by dry rot.
I would rather be a superb
meteor, every atom of me in
magnificent glow, than a sleepy
and permanent planet.
The function of man is to live,
not to exist. I shall not waste
my days in trying to prolong them.
I shall use my time.

Affirmation: I will live my life so that I have no regrets.

NAMASTE

June 10
Celebrating Our Children

"We find a delight in the beauty and happiness of children
that makes the heart too big for the body."
-Ralph Waldo Emerson

I've watched my children over the years—watched as they took their first steps and celebrated with them as they received their college degrees.

They never ceased to amuse and amaze me! My baby is fifty now and my eldest is fifty-four—hardly children anymore, and yet how precious is the memory of their "growing up."

My offspring are, and always have been, wiser than I ever was at their various ages and stages. During their lifetimes, as they have experienced hardships, both physically and emotionally, they did so, learning the secret of the alchemist—taking their times of lead and turning them into pure gold.

In his *Songs of Innocence*, William Blake said so perfectly what we mothers have always felt in wanting our children to be eternally safe and happy:

> When the voices of children are heard on the green
> And laughing is heard on the hill,
> My heart is at rest within my breast
> And everything else is still.

Affirmation: I thank God for my children, those unique expressions of love.

NAMASTE

June 11
Heaven on Earth

"The Father's kingdom is spread out upon the earth
and people do not see it."
-The Gospel of Saint Thomas

The seventeenth-century mystic, Jacob Boehme, said that "Heaven is throughout the whole world." More-and-more I believe him. All we have to do is tweak that "divine light" within us and we will see the Kingdom of God in everything that surrounds us.

For centuries, mystics from every tradition have told us that paradise is right here, right now, if you will but put on your "heavenly glasses" and see it.

Our capacity to live "heaven on earth" daily is wonderfully possible. It just means changing the way we look at things, the stories that we tell ourselves. Life is all about "how we perceive." We can look at the shadow side of things that happen to us or we can find the sunshine in the experiences that enter our lives.

It's a self-fulfilling prophecy whether we want to see "The Father's kingdom" from our eyes or from His.

Affirmation: I see my world as Heaven on earth.

NAMASTE

June 12
Vast Abundance

"Abundance is about looking at life and knowing that you have everything you need for complete happiness, and then being able to celebrate each and every moment on Earth."
-Wayne Dyer
Everyday Wisdom For Success

The hummingbird feeder on my front porch has become a bit of a battleground.

There is one small, winged creature who has decided that it belongs to him and him alone. Whenever other hummers come near, he swoops over from wherever he has been watching, and, chirping loudly, chases them away.

How sad that he has not learned to share. He spends his day watching that feeder when he could be flying about enjoying life in nature, then coming back periodically from his adventures to enjoy the sweet nectar from the feeder. His fear seems to be that there is not enough for both himself and the other hummingbirds, even though my husband keeps the feeder filled at all times.

This tiny bird perceives his world as one of lack rather than interpreting it as one of abundance.

How do you perceive your world?

Affirmation: I am cognizant of the vast abundance that surrounds me.

NAMASTE

June 13
The Infinite Harpist

"The magic fingers of the Infinite Harpist touch the strings of our lives and we pour forth the pure, sweet music of ourselves."
-Author

While sitting in a teahouse last week with my friend, Linda, and my husband, I listened to the captivating music of a harp. There is nothing as soothing as the sultry tones of that angelic-like, stringed instrument.

Closing my eyes, I visualized myself as a lovely, golden harp. I could feel the Beloved placing his hands on my strings as he played out the music of my life.

If I could but stand before God as this beautiful Celtic instrument and allow Him to stroke each chord, my music to the world would surely be a breathtaking melody.

Affirmation: I am a harp and God, the harpist.

NAMASTE

June 14

Everything's Coming Up Roses

"We see and feel what we choose to see and feel."
-Author

When my first husband was attending college in Berkeley, and I was working on-campus, we became friends with a student in one of Ed's engineering classes.

The young man had been born and raised in Berkeley and he had a grandmother who was sequestered in an assisted-living compound just outside of town.

Often, on a Sunday afternoon, my husband and I would join our friend to visit his grandmother.

This dear woman was in what we now call, a "state of dementia." For her, however, it was a "state of bliss."

Her room was wallpapered with pink, cabbage roses and next to her, at all times, lay a child's rag doll. When we entered her room, she would clap her hands and say, "Look what they did for dolly and me today, they planted a fresh garden of roses!"

For Grandma, waking up each morning included the joy of a newly planted garden of roses.

Our friend told us that, although his grandmother had always lived a humble life, void of material wealth, she had constantly found joy in each small thing. He said she had been happiest in her garden or walking in nature.

Through the years, how we view life will be exactly how we see it in our dotage—even in our dementia.

Affirmation: Daily, I will see my life as a proverbial rose garden.

NAMASTE

We Are Artists of Our Own Destinies

"I saw the angel in the marble and carved until I set him free."
-Michelangelo

Michelangelo believed that sculpture was the highest form of art. He compared it to divine creation, and claimed that he could actually see David inside the stone as he worked on the now famous Italian statue.

Like Michelangelo, we strive to chisel away the outer, useless rock of our lives, the purposeless material of hate, anger, unforgiveness and prejudice that does not serve us.

As we eliminate these useless bits of marble, we can then be transformed into the magnificent work of art that we truly are.

Affirmation: Like Michelangelo's David, I am a magnificent work of art.

NAMASTE

June 16

Keep Wearing Your Beautiful, Authentic Hat

"It is easy in the world to live after the world's opinion."
-Ralph Waldo Emerson

Wouldn't it be wonderful to always wear your favorite hat, the one that fits perfectly, the one that colorfully blends with your personality and your mood?

How many times do you change hats in order to please others— your husband, your boss, your friend or a family member? By the end of the day, after changing from a Stetson to a bonnet, a pillbox or a helmet, your hair is a mess and your brain is scrambled. You don't know who in the heck you are.

It's okay that others prefer different styles of hats, but that doesn't mean you have to keep changing yours in order to make them comfortable or to like you better.

Ralph Waldo Emerson wrote:

"What must I do is all that concerns me—not what people think.
It is easy in the world to live after the world's opinion; it is easy in solitude to live after our own; but the great man is he who in the midst of the crowd keeps with perfect sweetness the independence of solitude."

Affirmation: I will wear my own, perfect hat at all times.

NAMASTE

June 17
Starting Life Anew

"Live each day as if your life had just begun."
-Goethe

I have always been fond of the saying, "Today is the first day of the rest of your life." It has a "new beginning" feel to it, a potential for exciting opportunities and fresh, new experiences.

Take this day and see it as though it is a brand new life. How will you live it?

How will you fill these next twenty-four hours?

Picture your "new beginning" as a rollicking, joyous adventure and then go out and live it.

Affirmation: Today my life begins anew.

NAMASTE

June 18

Our Natural Essence

"There's a rhythm to the universe. When we're able to get quiet enough, we experience how we're a part of that perfect rhythm."
-Dr. Wayne W. Dyer
Staying on the Path

Sitting on my front porch in the moist air of an overcast day, I become the embodiment of its pure, cool essence. Like Buddha, Jesus and Gandhi, I yearn to align myself with the Greater Wellspring, to let my life and my love, like the damp air surrounding me, touch others in a way that will heighten the awareness of their own True Nature.

Within each of us, there abides a fundamental goodness that is the God-given substance of whom we truly are. How many of us recognize that goodness? How many of us express that goodness?

Walt Whitman wrote, "I am larger, better than I thought. I did not know I held so much goodness."

Affirmation: My true nature is that of love and goodness.

NAMASTE

June 19
What Now?

"But the path of the just [the caregiver] is as the shining light, that shineth more and more unto the perfect day."
-Proverbs 4:18

Many of us ask ourselves, "what now?" when we have been responsible for someone who has been ill for months, and sometimes years, and then they make their transition.

When our lives are preoccupied with care giving, we sometimes lose sight of our own identity—melt into the urgent needs of another. Through their death, we are relieved of those duties. We need to see this as God's way of leading us farther on our own spiritual journey.

"What now?" can first become a time of mourning and then a reflecting period of "who am I?" and "what do I want for myself?"

Open the door to several possibilities and then walk through the one that makes you smile, that feels deliciously exciting.

You're free to be you! Go, now, and enjoy that freedom.

Affirmation: I will enjoy my delightful freedom.

.

NAMASTE

June 20
Stare Awhile

"I have learned to look on nature . . . whose dwelling is the light of setting suns, and the round ocean and the living air, and the blue skies
-William Wordsworth

Punkie can sit for hours on our front porch glider and just stare off into space. Often, I'll put down my book or tablet and join her, following her gaze.

The hummingbirds suckling from the feeder become iridescent green and red focal points as do the myriad of birds flocking into our stone container filled with wild bird seed.

A cat meanders by and stops momentarily to stare at us; a lizard slithers out from under the maple tree to scurry across the garden.

We can see so much beauty and life when we stop long enough to stare.

John Wesley wrote, "I look upon the world as my parish."

I often wonder what sermons Punkie preaches from her front porch glider pulpit as she communes, eye-to-eye, with nature's congregation.

Affirmation: Today I will take time to just sit and stare.

NAMASTE

June 21

Summer Solstice

"Praise to thee, my Lord, for all thy creatures,
Above all Brother Sun
Who brings us the day and lends us his light.
-Saint Francis of Assisi

Today we are observing the Summer Solstice. It is a day of honoring the sun.

The word "Solstice" is derived from two Latin words: "sol," meaning sun, and "sistere," to cause to stand still. As the Summer Solstice comes near, the noonday sun rises higher and higher in the sky on each consecutive day. On the day of the Solstice, it rises so much higher than the day before that it seemingly stands still. Daytime hours are the longest in the Northern hemisphere, and night time is at a minimum.

Last evening, my husband and I attended a Summer Solstice drumming celebration.

We sat among Sycamore, Redwood, California Live Oak, Nottingham English Oak, Bunya Pine and Ornamental Plum trees while listening to the beat of fifty-or-so drums. Conga, Djembe, Tibetan Damaru, Bata ceremonial drums and even drums filled with beads that, when tipped back-and-forth, mimicked the ocean tides.

Children from two to sixteen years old beat on their own home-made tambours, decorated with colorful ribbons and bright beads.

Dogs barked with enthusiasm and people, young and old, danced to the rhythm of nature and drum.

After an hour or so, our leader gave each of us a piece of paper on which we wrote an intention for the year. Then he collected our papers and ceremoniously cast them into the flames of a large fire pit. The beating of drums and a chorus of chants accompanied the smoke and ashes spiraling upward to the Great Father.

I closed my eyes, letting the drums, bamboo rain sticks and rattles combined with the gentle breezes and tall trees embrace my soul, and I thanked Infinite Nature for the earth, the sun, the moon and the stars.

Following the sacred offering of our intentions, I became one with everything as the loud, ringing gong of a sacred Tibetan bowl filled the air around me.

Affirmation: I celebrate the Summer Solstice.

NAMASTE

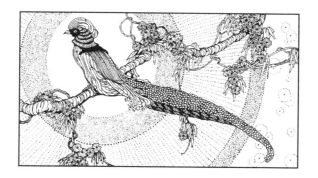

June 22
Sunshine and Candles

"As each of us finds peace in our own heart, we begin to radiate a light that warms and heals everyone we contact."

-Alan Cohen

Joy is my Compass

This morning when I awoke, I stared across at the dresser where I had placed a huge bouquet of mixed flowers the day before.

The vertical blinds in our bedroom were closed, but one of the slats was askew, letting in a small strip of shimmering sunlight. The way the sun fell across the bouquet made each flower blaze bright as though touched by fire. It was a magnificent sight and I lay there for a long time enjoying the small miracle before me.

How like that spray of flowers we can all be if we but allow the Infinite Sunlight to shine in us, on us and through us.

Before I started my writing this morning, I lit a small, lavender-scented candle and placed it on the table beside me. I often use the flame from a candle as a means of going into meditation. Staring at the flickering light quiets my mind and then I either stay still in open-eyed meditation or close my eyes for a deeper contemplation.

Light is abundant both in nature and in us as human beings. All we have to do is look for it to see the Infinite Light in all things and all people.

Affirmation: Today I look for the Light in everyone and everything.

NAMASTE

Releasing to Infinite Love

"The Almighty Healer reaches out to take your hand."
-Author
You say my family needs me
And I pour another drink.
You tell me my husband left
And I shoot another line.
You beg me to get out of bed
And I do, to snort some coke.
Then you whisper "God loves you so,"
And I lower the gun from my head.
-Author

It is three in the morning and I'm cradled here in my sanctuary chair after being awakened from a sound sleep with the words of the above poem racing through my mind, words like an urgent message begging to be sent, carried to someone in need of "the Infinite Healer."

Is today perhaps the day for one of you to begin that healing—to find the help you long for? And, most of all, to know that the God who created you and loves you so much has put within you the strength to make the right decision for your body, the strength to love yourself enough to walk that path of non-addiction. Please know, Dear One, that He will be with you each step of your journey to wholeness.

I have a precious step-daughter who walked through the valley of the shadow of addiction and then, turning to God, walked out of that dark place into the light of Infinite Love. Join her, won't you?

Affirmation: Today I release my addiction and seek the help I need, knowing that I am held close by the Almighty Healer.

NAMASTE

June 24
Accessing Your Inner Wisdom

"When you speak from your heart, everyone listens, because God is speaking."
-Author unknown

As I rest on my front porch this evening, I feel the deep serenity of a day well-spent, a day of accessing Divine Wisdom.

I have written long hours, not from my limited, human viewpoint, but through a mind centered on the presence of the God Author within.

Experience has shown me that when I listen to and follow the voice of the Beloved, my creative juices flow more freely through me and words miraculously place themselves on the page before me.

Writing becomes a deeply spiritual experience when I listen to the Infinite Scribe.

Affirmation: I access my Inner Wisdom.

NAMASTE

June 25
Come Fly With Me

"Come fly with me beyond the myth of self, into the truth
of All There Is."
-Author

The warm stillness on the front porch this morning is almost tangible, full of the mystery of the day.

Before me, my stone Buddha sits on his glass throne in quiet meditation, his background a vine of large green leaves and pink trumpets of mandevilla blossoms meandering back-and-forth on string between the columns of the porch.

Birds flit from branch to branch on one of the camphor trees as if begging me to join them—to play among the feathery leaves. There is a part of me that wants to fly off of my porch and join the high-spirited warblers.

I yearn to soar into the sky, the shadow of my great wings moving along the ground beneath me.

Over and over I hear in my mind the words, "You can fly, you can fly." And I can! I can unfold the wings of the Infinite Bird within, leaving behind the shallow shadow of myself, to soar into the sacred bliss of All There Is.

Affirmation: Today I will unfold my sacrosanct wings and fly.

NAMASTE

June 26

Receiving

"Never refuse the goodness that God has to offer."
-Author

No matter where your blessings come from—accept them.

If your children offer to pay for someone to come each month and clean your house, take that offer.

If a dear, human angel volunteers to have your carpets cleaned, thank God for it.

If someone wants to give you a special gift, take it.

When given a compliment, say "thank you."

It is through the circulation of giving and receiving that The Universe maintains its balance. Say "yes" to God's infinite source no matter which angel provides it.

Affirmation: With a thankful heart, I will both give and receive.

NAMASTE

Love—The Best Antidote For Fear

"Love is the warming and awakening of the soul."
-Author

For five years, in my early thirties, I lived mostly within the confines of my own home. Like the poet, Emily Dickinson, I rarely ventured out and when I did, panic would grab me like a hawk does its prey—suddenly and unexpectedly.

With the help of therapy, I slowly re-entered the outside world. And then, with the practice of doing what I call my "spiritual" work, reading, prayer and meditation, I came to understand that the best remedy for fear is love—pure and simple love.

I have spent the better part of this day sitting on my front porch, watching the buttery sunlight of afternoon turn into the silver-gray of dusk and then flow into the deep purple of night. Crickets have taken up their chirping, and gratitude, like the full moon above, lights up my world—gratitude for a God who led me from fear to love.

Love is the warming and awakening of the soul
The arms of a caring mother
The touch of the Beloved
The letting go of fear
-Author

Affirmation: In loving myself and others, I release all fears.

NAMASTE

June 28
Be Open to Everything

"I wish to say what I think and feel today, with the promise that
tomorrow perhaps I shall contradict it all."
-Ralph Waldo Emerson

I have changed my beliefs at least three times in the past seventy-six
years. And each conviction was so very right for me at the time.

My Spiritual paths have twisted and turned and yet, my holy walk
has been interesting, entertaining and beautiful in every aspect.

There is more than one path. Give yourself permission to explore
those off-road, exciting trails.

Affirmation: I can choose any and as many paths as I want.

NAMASTE

June 29

Beings of Light

"During each of our journeys, there are those inevitable moments
when someone [or something] comes into our life at precisely the
right time and says or does precisely the right thing."
-Madison Taylor
Daily OM

I had a disk challenge a few years ago that weakened my spine to the
point that I was unable to stand or walk.

Through exercises that I was able to do in my bed, my back
eventually became stronger and I ventured outside to walk, slowly and
carefully, up and down the sidewalk.

I started with just ten steps, fearing my back would collapse and I
would fall.

Then, as I gained confidence, I increased my steps to twenty.

I had been concentrating so hard on not falling that I was surprised
when I looked up and saw two dragonflies, one on either side of me.
Every time I turned, they turned with me. Back-and-forth we went
together, a wobbly woman and two precious angels disguised as
dragonflies. The confidence I gained from those two light workers was
wondrous.

When my husband came out on the porch, I pointed out the magic
phenomenon and he stood staring in disbelief, as, with each turn, the
dragonflies continued up and down the walk with me, never leaving
my side.

There are those moments in our lives when angels appear to help
us. Some are human, but, often, they are part of the animal or flora
kingdom.

Watch for the angels in your life. Ask for these angelic experiences.

Affirmation: I welcome angels into my life.

NAMASTE

June 30
Dance of the Birds

". . . The time of the singing of birds is come . . ."
-Song of Solomon 2:12

A feathered performance is being staged for me this morning. My special box-seating is my front porch and the stage for the production is the sky between my elm tree and my neighbor's flowering hibiscus.

The winged prima ballerinas soar from tree-to-tree, periodically floating down to alight on the bird feeder in my yard. Then, gracefully sweeping back into the air, they continue their elegant performance.

Instead of dancing to the music of The Sugar Plum Fairy, these artisans of the air pirouette to the song of the Universe—their own sweet trilling.

Affirmation: Birds dance and sing—I applaud nature in all its splendor.

NAMASTE

July 1

What is Our Abundance?

"My abundance is not limited to the amount of money I possess."
-Author

Today, I would like to share with you what abundance looks and feels like to me. After reading my list, make one of your own and add to it each day.

ABUNDANCE IS:

Sitting in my sanctuary in the evening with candles lit, reading poetry, listening to the bark of a far-away dog and the sounds of crickets in symphony. It is the touch of a silken breeze wafting through the open windows, gently caressing my skin.

ABUNDANCE IS:

Being with family and friends, sharing food, conversation and laughter.

ABUNDANCE IS:

Loving deeply and being deeply loved.

ABUNDANCE IS:

The passion I feel in writing—in co-creating with the Beloved.

ABUNDANCE IS:

The joy of financial freedom—the freedom to dance the good life and to share that financial tango with others

ABUNDANCE IS:

My welcoming front porch.

ABUNDANCE IS:

Living in a country that allows me to embrace whatever faith I choose and a Spiritual Center that encourages me to choose them all.

ABUNDANCE IS:

The constant knowing that I walk daily with the Internal Energy of Life—my Beloved.

Affirmation: Today I count the blessings of my abundance.

NAMASTE

July 2
Tara

"I am a strong, loving Tara force."
-Author

On the wall of my sanctuary, I have hung a small, exquisite porcelain bust of Tara. It is a work of art depicting the mother of all Buddha's—the feminine principle of the Buddha.

One legend of Tara is that she was born from a beautiful lotus. She does, in fact, sit on a lotus throne.

She is possibly the first feminist—a warrior goddess who fought against the cultural belief that women are subordinates.

Like other goddesses, Tara has taken on the job of ending the suffering of mankind. She is a completely selfless entity. Through her persona, we are reminded of other mythological goddesses. She has the motherly instincts of Demeter; the virgin beauty of Artemis; the wisdom of Athena; and the power of Innana. However, because she is a fully enlightened Buddha, she does not have the dark shadows of the human-like goddesses found in myth.

When we call out to her as a mother goddess, she sees us and responds as though each of us was her only, cherished child.

Affirmation: Each day I respond to my children as if I were Tara.

NAMASTE

July 3

Amazing Love

"What does love have to do with aging?
EVERYTHING!"
-Author

As we grow older, the need to cozy up to that most important of all emotions, love, becomes stronger.

We yearn to embrace the Infinite Caregiver within—to wrap our arms around the Beloved and breathe in the tender warmth of our Mother/Father God.

> To wait an Hour—is long—
> If love be just beyond—
> To wait eternity—is short—
> If Love reward the end—
>
> -Emily Dickinson

Affirmation: I breathe in the tender warmth of God.

NAMASTE

July 4
Liberty

"Proclaim liberty throughout all the land and with all the
inhabitants thereof."
-Leviticus 25:10

Today, on the 4th of July, we celebrate our independence and freedom from Great Britain.

The word "liberty" is actually a very personal word. A few years ago, I formed an acronym that pleases me each time that I repeat it. I share that with you now.

L   Living
I   In
B   Bright
E   Energetic
R   Relationship
T   To
Y   Yourself

We, in America, have been blessed with the ability to make our own choices, a freedom that many people in other countries do not enjoy. That macrocosmic freedom can most definitely trickle down to the microcosmic independence of individual choice.

Do you stand up for what you believe? Or, perhaps, you are allowing others to make your choices for you. If the latter is true for you, it might be time to "own your own power." Start today to live in the bright, energetic relationship to yourself.

Affirmation: Today, I begin to lovingly make my own decisions and celebrate the 4th of July every minute of my life.

NAMASTE

July 5

Predawn Bliss

"These quiet morning moments are precious points in one man's brief life, yet they are the essence of the eternal . . ."
W. Phillip Keller
Still Waters

It is five in the morning, just before daybreak. From my front porch the world before me lies etched in silver—the magnificent color of predawn.

It is the sacred hour of calm before life begins its busy day—before birds awaken, stretch their wings and warble a grand good morning to the Universe.

These still, early mornings are priceless to me, moments when God speaks longest. They are moments of being wrapped in the quiet pewter that surrounds me, leaving me breathless in the magic just before dawn.

Quietly, I say, "Thank you, God, thank you for the splendidness and grandeur of Your early morning and Your exquisite artistry of a landscape painted in silver love across the sky.

Affirmation: I will relish the silver magic before sunrise.

NAMASTE

July 6

Woe is Me

"Negativity creates more negativity that eventually
spawns a life of negativity."
-Author

How many times have you gone to a dinner party and found yourself sitting next to someone who loves to play "Ain't It Awful?"

"My kids never come to visit me."

"My job sucks."

"There's never enough money."

"The politicians all stink."

"The world is a mess."

That happened to me recently, and when the man finally stopped complaining long enough for me to speak, I looked him in the eye and said, "Now, tell me something wonderful that happened to you this week."

He stared back at me, mouth agape as if I had insulted him, as though I was an alien from mars, speaking an unknown, foreign language.

Without another a word, the poor guy turned back to his food and continued eating.

I refused to play his game and so our conversation was over.

Keep your thoughts and your words positive and watch your life change.

Affirmation: I will keep my thoughts and words positive.

NAMASTE

July 7
The Power of Positive Prayer

"And all things, whatsoever ye shall ask in
prayer, believing, ye shall receive."
-Matthew 21:22

How clear Christ was when he spoke the above words to his disciples. To me, the word "believing" is the key to prayer.

In the previous verse, Jesus said, "If you have faith and doubt not . . . ye shall say to this mountain, be thou removed, and be thou cast into the sea; it shall be done."

These powerful words show us that Christ knew we had the same energy that he possessed—all we have to do is truly believe in those God-given abilities.

Through prayer, we feel a beautiful connection to Infinite Love, as well as to those for whom we pray.

Take time right now to find the stillness within. Go back in this book to January 27 and follow the CALL method for prayer and then pray for a loved one, or maybe a difficulty that has come up in your life, and "believe" your positive words.

Affirmation: In prayer, I release all doubt, and, through my strong belief, I receive.

NAMASTE

July 8
You Are a Moment-by-Moment Creator

"We create our days one moment at a time."
-Author

My sister, Sally, and her husband, Duane, recently paid us a visit from the beautiful island of Hawaii. They usually make the flying trek once each year.

Our days together are spent wandering through shops, lingering over dinner at our favorite restaurants or enjoying candle-lit meals and conversation in our own dining room. We have even been known to sojourn down the freeway to the quaint town of Temecula, our favorite antique stomping grounds, where we load up the car with "old stuff" that we just can't live without.

Then there are the fun board games that we play in the evening hours accompanied by the laughter of "wrong moves made" and "sending our opponents back home."

What bliss it is to create, moment-by-moment, our own experiences, to share our days and our joys with those we love! We can then hold the memories of those shared times within our hearts until the next visit when, once again, we create new Universal moments.

Affirmation: I will take the time from my busy schedule to create those "cloud nine" moments.

NAMASTE

July 9

Stay in There

"You can have a disability and still stay in the game."
-Author unknown

I spent today, with a woman who is like a daughter to me—a delightful, intelligent woman who owns her own home and who keeps high standards for herself.

We went to an olive oil shop, a craft store, a grocery store specializing in organic foods and a new age gift shop. Then we had lunch at my favorite tea house (what tea house, I ask you, is not my favorite?)

This fascinating person with whom I leisurely idled away the day is a strong, resilient woman who has suffered her whole life with a slow-developing form of spinal muscular atrophy (SMA). It is a disease whose disabling symptoms often increase with age.

Has Sandy let this crippling disorder stop her?

Oh, no!

It has barely slowed her down. She has a high-profile position that consumes far more than eight hours a day and that often, takes her out in the evening for meetings with constituents. I attended one of those meetings with her, and boy, can she "work a room!"

Our disabilities don't have to stop our lives. It's our attitude towards those handicaps that bring us to a standstill.

Sandy not only lives her life to the fullest, but in every conversation with her, I have heard nothing but thankfulness for that full life.

Affirmation: I won't let my disability take me out of the game.

NAMASTE

July 10
The Miracle of Being Fully Alive

"The glory of God is found in the person who is fully alive."
-St. Irenaeus
Fourth-century Mystic

What does it mean to be "fully alive?"

To me, it means a life surging with bliss, passion, love and an enthusiasm for living so great that I can't wait to take my next breath.

We all need to recognize the miracles in our lives, everyday miracles such as waking up each morning, eating nourishing food, holding a puppy or a baby in our arms, or picking a bouquet of roses.

Often we equate miracles with spontaneous healings or winning the lottery, but truly, everything in our lives constitutes a miracle, no matter how large or small that phenomenon appears.

As you walk your daily life, look about and thank God for all the miracles that surround you. Become fully alive to a universe that the Beloved has created just for you.

Affirmation: My life is overflowing with miracles.

NAMASTE

July 11
We Are All Scholars

"There is a wisdom of the head, and . . . a wisdom of the heart."
-Charles Dickens

Today, after attending a class at my Spiritual Center where everyone participated in a lively discussion, my friend, Susan, mentioned how much she enjoyed learning from others.

Later, after thinking about her comment, I realized how truly wonderful it is to learn laterally—to be taught by each other. When we share our life's lessons in a group, we learn collectively, for we are each scholars in our own rights.

Every one of us is an expression of the Infinite Professor, and the knowledge that we have garnered from Him, we can pass on to each other.

Affirmation: I enjoy learning laterally.

NAMASTE

July 12
Compassionate Listening

"If you only listen with your head, the words will only go as far as your
ears. If you listen with love, the words go to your heart."
-Sufi saying

The talk Reverend Danell Wheeler gave on Sunday at the Spiritual Center
where I attend services was so beautiful that, with her permission, I
now share parts of it with you.

"Compassionate listening is a wonderful tool for many things:
conflict resolution; reconciliation with relationships; and prevention of
aggressive behavior—to name but a few.

"This mode of listening necessitates being completely and absolutely
present in the current moment with the person who is talking. It means
listening without judgment and without interrupting. It's about keeping
your focus on the one who is speaking and not indulging in the urge
that we have to share our own stories, our own personal experiences or
to offer that unsolicited suggestion or advice because 'we know what's
best for them.'

"So many times, people want nothing more than to be heard and,
in that process of being heard, they discover their own answers. Don't
you find that you do that, too? By talking to yourself, "bouncing it off
the wall" so to speak, you find yourself saying 'Ah, there it is! That's the
answer I was looking for! Gee! It was within me all the time!'

"Compassionate listening is not about sharing what "I" know. It's
about helping others make that realization about what they know as
they speak. Being this kind listener provides an absolute love presence.
It's about expressing your divinity and just being. It is our life's work to
practice that 'being present'—to learn how to see others from their own
eyes rather than from our own conditioned perceptions and judgments.
And, with that open-mindedness, we grow and we obtain a deeper
understanding of life.

"When we can listen to others from that place of compassion, we are honoring that person. We are validating that person who is speaking.

"Listening—being fully present—is hugely about respect. It's about completing that circle of giving and receiving. It enables us to open up our hearts unconditionally."

Affirmation: I am a compassionate listener.

NAMASTE

July 13

Imagination

"Only through imagination can we truly see the world."
-Author

Don't you just love to use your imagination?

When I put my "imagination DVD" into play, I see a movie where all of the people in the world stand hand-in-hand in a large circle singing, "Let there be peace on earth and let it begin with me," that beautiful song by Jill Jackson Miller.

I see people listening to each other "compassionately," and treating each other with high regard and much love.

I watch the screen as all manifestations of life live together in stability and order and all flora and fauna are allowed to grow and thrive, burgeoning and blooming.

Close your eyes and let your imagination flow, bringing forth whatever it is you seek for yourself and for the world. Doing this can bring you such joy!

Affirmation: Whatever I imagine can become a reality.

NAMASTE

July 14
The Dawning of Love

"The canine [Nandhi] watched this exchange between the two monks and sensed, for the first time, a feeling growing in his heart that he had never experienced before. He could not say what it was other than it felt very good—very warm. Perhaps it was love."
-Craig Steven Phillips
The Buddha's Dog

The Buddha's Dog is a book for children from the ages of eight to one-hundred-and-eight. It is a beautiful tale of an abandoned dog who must steal food in order to survive; a canine with a roguish personality—until he comes upon the Great Buddha.

Like gravity and electricity, the emotion of love is a force so mighty, so potent, that though its energy cannot be seen, still it abides in each of us. Love is the most powerful, beautiful emotion that we possess.

Prentice Mulford wrote, "Love is an element which though physically unseen is as real as air or water. It is an acting, living, moving force . . . it moves in waves and currents like those of the ocean."

When we learn to love ourselves and others, we invite those same deep feelings to flow through us and to us.

Robert Browning said, "Take away love and our earth is a tomb."

Relax, now, and close your eyes. When ready, repeat the following mantra as many times as needed. "Fill Me with radiating love."

The warmth and joy that you will experience welling up from deep inside of you is love—love that might well bring you to tears.

Affirmation: I will allow myself to feel and express the radiating warmth of love.

NAMASTE

July 15
We Must Go Through It

"While we may not be able to control all that happens to us, we can control what happens inside us."
-Benjamin Franklin

This afternoon, I am neither sitting on my front porch nor am I in my sanctuary.

Actually, I'm lying flat on my back in my bed having just come from the doctor with a diagnosis of strained tendons, sprained muscles and torn ligaments in my back. All of this simply because I forgot I wasn't twenty years old and decided that I needed to move furniture and books in my living room because the "chi" needed to flow more evenly. (So much for feng shui.)

This is, yet again, another of my "metaphorical moments" of just "being." And, since I can only sit up for half an hour at a time, I am composing this vignette via a tape recorder. It is probably how I will be writing this book for the next month.

Is it a tragedy? Oh, no! It's just another plan that the Beloved has for my life. We all have times of suffering, either physical or emotional, and, in these moments, we need to know that Spirit is with us and that everything is in perfect order.

I have a friend who is going through her own challenge. She is a dear woman whose daughter will soon be leaving to attend college in another state. My friend's pain is no different from mine. It is equally as intense. She and her daughter are like the mother and daughter in the TV series, The Gilmore Girls. In their closeness, they experience great joy in being together. Now this parting, like my torn ligaments, is so very painful. I have put her in my "prayer pot" and she, as always, has put me in hers. That's what loving each other through our "dark nights of the soul" is all about.

When we have any kind of pain, we cannot go under it, over it, or around it, we simply must go through it—there is no other way. And, in so doing, we grow—oh, how we grow!

My dear husband has now taken over all of the household chores, and I, like The Princess and the Pea, lie here in my uncomfortable bed, being waited on hand-and-foot. He, too, has had times of suffering in his life and so he knows and understands my distress. How wonderful is that?

On the first day of my challenge, I thanked God for it, recognized it, and shouted to the Universe how much I didn't want it. And then I settled down in my bed to willingly just "be."

Affirmation: I will not go under, over, or around my pain, I will go through it; knowing that it will better enable me to love others through their pain.

NAMASTE

July 16
The Best is Yet to Be

"Grow old along with me."
-Robert Browning

I am just beginning to thaw from the icy grief of loss—loss of who I was before the age of seventy and all that it represents—something that I didn't let myself acknowledge until this morning while lying in my bed: joints that were lithe and moved easily, eyes that saw more clearly, legs that could walk and run for miles and a back that was strong and resilient are all a thing of the past.

But, now, as I dig deeper into what aging really means, I realize that the imaginary pool beneath my feet—the thawing of icy grief—is a glistening lake of wisdom, love and resilience that only almost eight decades of living could have spawned.

Today I opened my arms to a God that is more than sufficient to dance with me through my 80s, 90s and 100s.

My grief turns to pure joy when I realize that, as Robert Browning said:

"Grow old along with me!
The best is yet to be,
The last of life for which the first was made."

So now I know that the only reason for living through my youth and middle age was to be here in the best part—here and through to my hundredth birthday!

Affirmation: I know that whatever age I am, "The best is yet to be."

NAMASTE

July 17
Rejoicing in What Is

"It is during the challenging times of our lives that we
grow into full comprehension."
-Author

I rest on my front porch this morning, taking my "allowed half hour of sitting" to enjoy the silence of the predawn.

A drake flies overhead on his way to the pond behind my house, his loud squawk heralding the new day.

Punkie lies on a blanket at my feet gazing up with soulful eyes, probably wondering why she can't be in her appointed place beside me on the glider. In my present state, I am simply not able to bend over and pick her up.

I allow myself a quick, five-second "pity party" and then remember that it is in our challenges that we become quiet, that we pause to watch the duck, the birds and the lizard go skittering and flying by. It is a time of stilling our minds and listening to the sounds of nature and the voice of the Beloved.

Now, I gaze up in awe as the rising sun bursts through the hovering clouds, lighting them as though set off by a fiery torch, and the sky becomes an artist's palette of vibrant pinks, causing me to gasp at the grandeur and magnificence of our vast universe.

It is then that I thank God for allowing me this space of just "being" so that I have the time to soak up all of the beauty and splendor of His creation.

Affirmation: I thank God for my times of just "being."

NAMASTE

July 18

Looking at Life From the Inside

"In meditation we go to our heart center and follow the breath. The answer to all questions lies within, and when we persevere in meditation and prayer, we will receive our answer."
-Gail Manishore
From Here to Serenity

How does life look to you? If your answer is that it's a dark, troubled or fearful place, then it's time to go within and access your "real" world.

When we close our eyes and capture the essence of God, our universe just naturally arcs into a colorful rainbow of love and peace. We find ourselves in tune with our original bliss and feel the beating pulse of Infinite Life.

The more time we spend in the quiet solitude of communion with the Beloved, the more our lives expand into new and broader dimensions.

Right now, close your eyes and ask Divine Source to fill you with light and peace, then let your day mirror that essence—the essence of Who You Really Are.

Affirmation: My world is a serene place of love and peace.

NAMASTE

July 19
Soulmaking

"Call the world, if you please, the vale of soulmaking."
-John Keats

Outside, today, the heat hangs in the air in a suffocating blanket of moist humidity.

For me, it is a time of hermitting within the four walls of my cool, air-conditioned home, doing what I like to call "soulmaking," a period of growing my inner spirit. I will experience hours when, as Meister Eckhart writes, "Everything tastes like God."

I will listen to my soul, that spark of the Divine within me, that Powerful Creative Force, and, for the rest of this summer afternoon, I will simply stay in the moment, one long, unending, sacred moment of peace and tranquility.

Affirmation: This is a perfect day for "soulmaking."

NAMASTE

July 20
Unplug!

"Stop talking, stop thinking, and there is nothing you will not
understand."
-Jianzhi Sengcan

I was scheduled this week-end to attend a two-day silent retreat at a
Spiritual Center in the beautiful pine-forest mountains of Idyllwild.

Owing to the fact that I have torn the ligaments in my back, and that
I cannot sit for two hours in a car, I will be doing my silent "retreating"
here at home.

It is so important in this modern day of technology to periodically
turn off our computers, our iPods and our cell phones—to silence our
"blueberries," or "gooseberries," or is it "blackberries?" (It's some kind
of berry!)

It is equally as important to teach our "techno-youth" to learn how
to talk face-to-face with each other, sing and laugh together and, most
of all, to sit in silence and let the clear, sweet thoughts and voice of
Infinite Peace wash over and through their impressionable minds.

Affirmation: For one day, I turn off everything "technological" and
enjoy the silence.

NAMASTE

July 21
I'm Here for You

"Make yourself necessary to someone."
-Ralph Waldo Emerson

How many ways are there to say, "I'm here for you?"

Within the everyday circumstances of our lives, there are numerous opportunities for us to reach out and help someone.

The very fact that "we are all one," gives us the opportunity to lighten the burden of those around us, to reach out and express our love and caring in some way that will brighten their day. By valuing others, we are valuing ourselves in the process.

Become a passionate listener to someone who has lost a loved one. Provide food for a shut-in or a homeless person on the street, drive a friend to the doctor or, maybe, baby-sit for a young mother.

Whatever destiny presents, welcome it with open arms and an open heart.

Affirmation: I will make myself available to someone who needs me.

NAMASTE

July 22

Burgeoning Youth

"There was a child went forth every day,
And the first object he look'd upon, that object he became.
The horizon's edge, the flying sea-crow,
The fragrance of salt march and shore mud,
These became part of that child who went forth every day,
And who now goes, and will always go forth
Every day."
-Walt Whitman

This piece is dedicated to you, my beloved grandchildren and great-grandchildren.

Our children today represent not only our future but also an advancing expansion of human consciousness. They are more accepting of color, creed and homosexuality. Left alone, they see these things as "non-issues."

More than ever, our youth are involved in global change, the challenge of a planet in chaos. We have young people engaged in elephant rescue in Thailand, in orphanages throughout the world, and, here at home, they have involved themselves in Habitat for Humanity.

We have a generation with the ability to take the action of love and use it to change our world.

We, as adults, can give our youngsters strong and positive reminders of who they are. We can be diligent in looking for and praising the good that they do and seeing them as the perfect children of God that they are.

As we encourage our children in their vision for success, we can step aside and watch them heal the world!

Affirmation: With our help and their natural ability to love, our children can change the world.

NAMASTE

July 23
A Comfortable Party of One

"One of the greatest necessities in America is
to discover creative solitude."
-Carl Sandburg

During this time of confinement, I find myself quite pleased with my solitude—that comfortable "party of one." It has allowed me the time to think and formulate my thoughts and words.

While reposing quietly in my bed, I pick up my magic "talking machine" and dictate, letting the words of the Infinite Scribe pour through me.

It takes time and much mulling to write, and, through an injured back, Spirit has afforded me the space to answer the calling of my soul.

I am choosing to feel blest that I don't have to get dressed and go to work. My office is my Zen bedroom and my bed, a four-poster desk.

And, let me tell you, I have never felt more vigorous or more optimistic than during these last couple of weeks lying here on my four-poster desk, listening to the Beloved as he whispers magical words into my ear.

Affirmation: I take time to answer the calling of my soul.

NAMASTE

July 24
Comedy or Tragedy?

"Paint the tragedy side of your mask white, and you'll spend
the rest of your days smiling."
-Author

Today I came across an old program from a theater production that I
attended a few years back. Displayed on the cover of the program was
a picture of a comedy-tragedy mask where one half of the mask is black
and frowning and the other side, white and smiling.

I compared that mask to the choices that I can make during my
current "back challenge" and my forced exile from the outer world.

If I hold on to the "poor me," the dark side of the mask, I close myself
off from fully accessing the goodness of the Beloved. But if I count my
blessings, such as more time to read, more time to write, more time to
meditate and pray, then I see only the light side of the mask.

So, with imaginary canvas, pencil and paint, I create the same mask
that is shown on the cover of my program and then paint both sides
white and smiling. Yippee! Much better!

Affirmation: With the knowledge of God's constant presence in my life,
I live the comedy side of the mask.

NAMASTE

July 25

Joy

"Joy is the dance of a life well lived."
-Author

This morning I am listening to Megon McDonough. The words she is singing penetrate my very soul. "The joy is in the journey," are lyrics that can ring true for every single one of us.

While strolling upon this earth each day, we can make the elixir of our lives richer, lighter, and more flavorful when we walk in joy. Like lava from an erupting volcano, joy brings us to the brink of happiness— happiness that spills over and onto every sentient being around us.

Joy is the dance of a life well lived, the rhythm of co-creation with God, the beat of a heart open to everyone and everything.

Joy, like the autumn winds, scatters our golden leaves of delight and bliss to the four corners of our world.

Make your today a joyful one!

Affirmation: Today, I will bring joy to myself and others.

NAMASTE

July 26
The Insanity of War

"War isn't art, it's psychosis."
-Pursah
-Gary Renard
The Disappearance Of The Universe

Someone mentioned the other day that there is a book entitled *The Art of War*. Now, there's an oxymoron! I, for one, have yet to see how wars settle anything for very long, if ever. Fighting only brings about death and devastation. What kind of art is that? Many have said that war will bring us freedom. Non-violence, however, is the true path to freedom.

The following Zen story shows how senseless warfare is:

Behind a temple was a vine with many squashes growing on it.

One day a fight broke out among them, and the squashes split up into angry groups, making a big racket. Hearing the uproar, the head priest went outside, saw the quarreling, and scolded them: "Hey! Squashes!

Why are you fighting? Now—everybody do zazen."

The priest taught them how, teaching them to fold their legs and sit up straight. As the squashes began to follow the priest's instructions, they calmed down and stopped fighting.

"Now," the priest said, "everyone put your hand on top of your head."

When the squashes felt the top of their heads, they found something attached there. It was the vine that connected them all together.

"What a mistake!" the squashes cried out. "We're actually all connected, living just one life!"

From that moment on, the squashes never fought again.

Affirmation: I am a human squash connected to everyone else by the sacred vine of God.

NAMASTE

The Commonality of Breath

"One race there is of men, one of gods, but from one
mother we both draw our breath."
-Pindar

As I sat in meditation this morning, I realized that with each inhale and each exhale, every sentient being on earth, human as well as animal, and plant life, was breathing at the same time—in unison—as one.

WOW!

This thought brought me to a fuller realization of the meaning of "oneness." God is breathing us all in unity.

Today, feel the oneness, the sanctity of breath.

Affirmation: I am breathing in rhythm to every sentient being on earth.

NAMASTE

July 28
Be Still

"Today, and for all my tomorrows, I travel through this incredible life
on a journey filled with awe and wonder."
-Nancy Nisonger

My dear prayer-partner and friend, Nancy Nisonger, shared with me today this beautiful prayer and I pass it on to you.

"I breathe in and relax, feeling a sense of serenity and calm wash over me. As I bathe in this healing moment, I am restored to wholeness. I know I have lived each day to the best of my ability, and I feel the loving presence of Spirit.

In this stillness, my senses are hushed and I am aware of the ONENESS. I have an enlightened moment as I see my highest good opening like a sun-kissed flower before me, right HERE, and right NOW.

Today, and for all my tomorrows, I travel through this incredible life on a journey filled with awe and wonder. I know that You are with me every step of the way as my guide, and I am loved, protected and prosperous. Thank you, Dear Sweet Spirit, for the never-ending supply of goodness that overflows my entire being.

All that I am, and all that I do, I attribute to You. I give thanks for Your flowing source of Creativity, for Your Love, and for the Eternal Flame that never goes out. For when this journey ends, another begins. I am ONE in the Circle of Light.

And so I say, thank you, thank you, Mother, Father God!"

Affirmation: My stillness heightens my senses of wonder and goodness.

NAMASTE

July 29
Shimmering Stars of God's Everyday Miracles

"Go and catch a falling star . . . ."
-John Donne

Tonight I have plugged in the tiny, white lights strung on the potted trees resting on my front porch, and have lit the large candles sitting on the tables.

Looking upwards toward the sky, I see the half-circled, iridescent moon and fantasize taking the spoon from my finished ice cream bowl and flying up to sit on the moon's rounded edge. There, I ladle up thousands of stars and toss them down to earth like sparkling confetti being thrown from skyscraper windows onto a parade. Then I watch as my stars land one-by-one into the hands of those in need of a miracle and observe their miracles come true.

Matthew 7:7 reads, "Ask, and it shall be given you; seek and ye shall find; knock and it shall be opened unto you."

With those words, God throws down to us the most brilliant stars of all!

Affirmation: I claim God's miraculous stars!

NAMASTE

July 30
The Palette of Life

"But Phyllida, my Phyllida!
Her color comes and goes;
It trembles to a lily-
It wavers to a rose."
-Henry Austin Dobson

For me, growing older is a step-by-step journey; a journey that contains every color, shade, and nuance on the palette of life. We all choose those pastels and primaries each day that we live.

Today I want to be an ever-so-soft pink, a whispering shade that floats like a cloud through an azure sky—zephyr-like and gentle. I want to be blown by the winds of happenstance, floating wherever Infinite Life chooses, enjoying the adventure of it; nothing contrived—no preordained sense to it—just free-floating and light.

In this space, I can feel the shingles of fear and worry gently falling from the roof of my existence and, in their place, a soft, woven mat of green grass covers me. A mat that is cool and moist with the life-force of energy and love. I am wrapped in the safety of God. Like corn, I am protected by the Almighty Husk of Spirit.

I want to sing and dance within that Caring Energy, never worrying about "What If," only knowing the constant protection of "What Is"—that peaceful serenity of the "I Am" of life—the joy of being a remarkable soul within a remarkable body.

I am both involved and evolving, and the path will continue until I expand into that last portion of my existence when I become, once again, pure, golden soul.

Affirmation: Every day I experience a new Divine color.

NAMASTE

July 31
We're All at Least 50 Carats

"A diamond is a chunk of coal that made good under pressure."
-Anonymous

I woke up this morning feeling like a shimmering diamond—at least 50 carats!

Being curious as to how that particular metaphor popped into my mind, I had my husband go on-line in order to access my "diamondness."

It was interesting to find that the word "diamond" comes from the Greek word, "adamas," which means "indestructible."

Aha! That's what Spirit was telling me! Even though I have to dictate my book into a recorder and then stand at my computer with my keyboard raised on a small stool, I'm still able to keep writing in spite of, or maybe because of an injured back.

Hey! I'm indestructible!

The next interesting bit of information I learned from the article was that there are 4 c's to a diamond and, in reading about the 4 c's, I found myself comparing a diamond to us as human beings.

1. Carat: Carat is the unit of measurement used for a diamond. There are all sizes of diamonds, some are small, some large. Aren't we the same?

2. Color: Most people think diamonds are colorless, or white. That's because those are the diamonds that most retailers sell. However, these gems do come in colors of yellow, brown, pink, red, blue, purple, green, black, gray, violet and orange. We, as human beings, also come in many wonderful colors.

3. Cut: Diamonds are cut into various shapes. There is the oval, the round, the pear and the emerald cut, to name but a few. We, too, come in various shapes.

4. Clarity: This is my favorite of the 4 c's! Clarity is the degree to

which a diamond is free of blemishes and inclusions: blemishes being external—scratches and nicks and inclusions being within the stone—breaks and feathering. This is where we differ from the diamond. We can choose our clarity. By changing our external blemishes—our words and actions, and our internal inclusions—our thoughts and our feelings, we can make of ourselves a perfect, brilliant diamond.

It was a simple piece of carbon, after all, that turned itself into a radiant diamond!

Affirmation: I am a diamond of perfect carat, color, cut and clarity.

NAMASTE

August 1

Listen to Your Intuition

"The things we know best are those we have not learned."
Lue de Clapiers,
Marquis de Vauvenargues

Intuition is described in the dictionary as:

1. Immediate apprehension by the mind without reasoning.
2. Immediate apprehension by a sense.
3. Immediate insight.

We all possess intuition to some degree or another. It's not a psychic thing; it's just being open in our everyday lives to a "knowing without knowing how we know."

A few months ago, my husband and I were walking down a hallway toward our dentist's office and suddenly I was hesitant about getting into that dental chair—let me add, more hesitant than usual. I'm never thrilled about a trip to the dentist. I felt like we were going to have an earthquake and, at the same time, felt foolish for the thought.

I got through my procedure just fine, went home and, then, at noon, my house started to shake and things flew off of shelves. We were having an "off the Richter scale" quake.

When you have a strong sense of not wanting to get on a flight, take an earlier or a later plane. Learn to tune-in to your intuition. It's not paranoid, it's just listening.

Affirmation: I am an intuitive human being.

NAMASTE

August 2
A Tooth Fairy Sighting

"The joy of childhood need not end."
-Author

The traffic was heavy as I maneuvered my car through downtown San Diego. The year was 1965 and my then three-and-a-half-year-old son sat quietly in the back seat. I imagined he was contemplating the conversation we had just finished about his older sister who had recently lost a front tooth and had been visited by the tooth fairy.

We stopped at a red light next to a station wagon. Suddenly, my little boy came to life as he pointed toward the other car shouting, "Look, mommy, look! There's a whole car full of tooth fairies!"

Turning my head, I smiled and waved at the six nuns in their white summer habits. The windows of their car were open as were ours, so they had obviously heard Michael's exuberant words. There they sat, laughing and waving at my son.

That was a day that I will cherish forever. How wonderful to be able to share in our children's adventures.

Affirmation: I will take time to listen to my children and share in their childhood.

NAMASTE

We Are All Creations of God

"Each one of us emerged from a beautiful concept in the mind of God"
- Author

My life has been filled with ups and downs and darks and lights. I've come a long way over a sometimes bumpy road—bumps born of my own making as well as those simply created by life.

Now I'm at a time of just "being"—being who I really am: a mother, a wife, a grandmother, a great-grandmother, a writer, and, best of all, a divine concept in the mind of God who so wanted that beautiful idea to become a reality that She created me.

This vision thrills me! I like being a person that the Beloved just had to create.

You are the same, dear reader. You started out as a divine idea in the mind of God who so loved you and so wanted you to become a vibrant reality that She added flesh and bone to your soul.

Affirmation: Today I thank God for creating me.

NAMASTE

Antiquing

"I am not one who was born in the possession of knowledge; I am one who is fond of antiquity and earnest in seeking it there."
-Confucius

Where can you find a taste of life that encompasses hundreds of years and provides countless hours of entertainment?

Antiquing does that for me. It's my addiction of choice. Each piece in the store takes on a life of its own as my overactive imagination swoops back in time. The shop comes alive. Eighteenth-century ladies in billowing skirts pour tea from delicate Limoges teapots, and recline on satin Victorian fainting couches while reading the love poems of Elizabeth Barrett Browning. I can close my eyes and picture each nuance of that long ago, simpler era.

A few years back, this seasoned antiquer discovered what all seekers of heirlooms only hope for—a fabulous find! There is a series of children's books written in the 1930s that were read to me as a child. Each story was a tale of triplets whose names were Snipp, Snapp and Snurr. My mission was to find a copy and add it to my vast collection of children's books.

The search took months. Then one day, while browsing through a shop of rare books, I found it. Delighted beyond words, I grabbed the book from the shelf, glancing at the price tag as I walked toward the cash register. My enthusiasm paled as I read the price; $165.00 was a tad more than my budget would allow, so I sadly put it back on the shelf.

At this point the mission became a challenge. I was determined to find what had now become a rare out-of-print edition at a price I could afford.

The quest ended when, during one of my antiquing forays, I was sifting through a table of old books. As I put one aside to see what was underneath, there lay the same Snipp, Snapp and Snurr I had discovered a short time before.

My heart thumped wildly as I lifted it to check the price. The tag read $7.50! Now, the trick was to remain calm and get out of the store before someone found out how truly valuable the book was. Smiling innocently, I handed my money to the clerk, then turned and bolted out the front door.

My husband, who was sitting on a bench outside of the store, looked totally bewildered when his normally calm, demure, white-haired wife suddenly kicked up her heels and performed the touchdown victory dance on the sidewalk in front of the whole world.

Have I aroused your curiosity? Are you perhaps grabbing the keys to your car and heading for the nearest house of antiquities? If so, I'm delighted.

Welcome, my friend, to the wonderful world of yesterday.

Affirmation: I will visit an antique store and enter the marvelous past.

NAMASTE

August 5
The Joy of Writing

"Many believe—and I believe—that I have been designated for this work by God. In spite of my old age, I do not want to give it up; I work out of love for God and I put all my hope in Him."
-Michelangelo

Writing is that soul within me that demands its own life. Through it I capture bright sparks of feelings, actions and dialogue between people. How many parts of myself are there that can be played out on sheets, even reams of paper.

Sometimes as I write, shapes, forms and personalities begin to appear and a tale starts to spin like the web of a fast-working spider, weaving in and out toward a completed work of art.

At times, the canvas of my mind is blank. This is when I pick up a pen as I would a brush, and a lovely painting of thoughts and words fill the empty space, bringing with it that powerful adrenaline rush that only creativity can produce. I'm sure it carries the same excitement I might feel if I won the lottery. Instead of money, however, my marvelous reward is the stream of words falling from my mind onto the page beneath my pen. It's a glorious mixture of mind and Spirit uniting and giving birth to those sonnets and tales that lie dormant within each of us.

No one is without a story or a poem just waiting to be brought into existence.

Affirmation: I, too, have a story or a poem inside, waiting to be written.

NAMASTE

Dancing With the Fairies

"That fairy kind of writing which depends only upon
the force of imagination."
-John Dryden

I have always been intrigued by fairies. I dream of them, I yearn to dance with them, and so I wrote a poem about them.

Fairy Dance

Once long ago, a Princess so lovely
Went walking the gardens of Erin.
Her hair was the color of strawberry jam;
A gown of green silk she was wearin'.

The midsummer day was aglow with the light
Of the sun shining down on the moor;
When fairies appeared with gossamer wings
Soft dresses of bluebells they wore.

Dance with us please they called out with joy,
Come pirouette, frolic and sing.
Tapping her toes, she joined the wee group
Round and round in a bright fairy ring.

The whirling continued till setting of sun;
Ere long the lassie slept sound.
Covering her with a blanket of moss
The sprites then flew heaven-bound.

Goodnight, blessed child, they called from above
May your dreams contain flower and fern.
Be filled with joy as you go through your life
And keep watch for our magic return.

Affirmation: My life is filled with visions of fairies, flowers and fern.

NAMASTE

Summertime and the Livin' is Easy

"With the heat of a summer day comes the warmth of God's love."
-Author

The last few days have been so hot that I am forced to stay inside with the A/C on.

This morning, I ventured out early. I like to spend the mornings and evenings on my front porch. I need my time with the flora and the fauna! The hummingbirds dive-bomb me with their loud chirping because their feeder is empty. As hot as it is, I'm sure they need their liquid food.

The vapid heat seems to still the atmosphere. The absence of a breeze brings with it a quiet, solitary feeling. I am alone in the warming day, sitting on my porch, listening to the sounds of silence, inundated by the warmth of God's peace.

Today, life is perfect, my beloved front porch is perfect and the world is in the hands of the Perfect Creator.

Affirmation: The heat of summer brings with it the warmth of God's peace.

NAMASTE

August 8

Living our Truth

"We are all individuals contributing to the collective whole."
-Author

I feel that I was put on this earth to exhibit "that who I am"—that wonderful expression of God-In-Me.

What does God-In-Me feel like? What can I do to be that flesh-covered, walking, talking emissary of the Beloved? How can I live my truth as I know it without stepping on the toes of others who are, in turn, living their truth as they know it?

I believe I am here for a purpose. There is not another person in the world exactly like me. Within me lives the Essence of God, making me a unique expression of that best part of who I am.

We are all here as individuals to contribute to the collective whole. Each of us was given this life in order to express our God-given talent, then, hand-in-hand, expression-by-expression, we have the combined power to create a world of love, beauty and peace.

It is through unconditional love and respect that we can live and enjoy our own individual truths, at the same time respecting the truth of others as they see it.

Giving up judgment of other's beliefs that are unlike our own can turn our lives and our world around, making it a heaven on earth.

Affirmation: I live my truth as I know it, allowing others to do the same.

NAMASTE

August 9
Those Special Someones

"Friendship, like a treasured antique, becomes more
precious with time and care."
- Author

Where would we be if we didn't have those "special someones" in our lives, those friends who know our "uglies" and our "pretties" and still love us?

The Beloved is my ultimate friend, but there are times when I yearn to "talk it out," whatever "it" might be. I yearn to share my "stuff," loving and trusting that person with whom I am sharing—always that.

I find that the more people I come to love and trust, the more others just like them appear in my life.

When we learn to set aside our judgments of others and see them through Spirit's eyes (remember, we are all soul-connected), then we get to view them as they are—perfect in every way.

Affirmation: As I ask for loving friends, the Beloved brings them to me.

NAMASTE

Romantic Relationships

"A romantic relationship is two people dancing in mutual rhythm."
-Author

Relationships can teach us who we truly are. They are a training ground to learn what we want and don't want in a partner. Then we can either stay with that person or move on. The journey is always the lesson.

At times, a change can feel like a small death because it is the end of who we are, and, once again, the beginning of who I am.

When what you have in a relationship doesn't quite fit, you can go within to that quiet place and ask, "What do I want in a partner?" It is never about the other person, it is always about you. You cannot love and respect anyone else until you love and respect yourself.

Sit down and make a list of your needs, and then, in a short statement, define that need.

Part of my list was:

Need I need freedom and time to be alone.
Statement: I will find someone who will allow me time by myself and the freedom to be with others of my choice.

Need: I need to dance through life, not dawdle.
Statement: My partner will enjoy the dance of life.

Need: I need lots of friends of all ages.
Statement: My significant other will not be jealous of my friends. He will accept the fact that I might even talk to total strangers.

Need: I need oodles and oodles of books.
Statement: I will find someone who will allow me to spend our last

$20.00 on a book. (This one was very important to me!)

Remember, every relationship choice that we make affects the course of the rest of our lives.

Choose carefully! I did. His name is Bill.

Affirmation: I will discover who I am and what I need and then choose the right partner.

NAMASTE

August 11
Give Me Five

"Five times a day I will celebrate God in me."
-Author

In Libya, where 97 percent of the people are Islamic, there is the tradition of the daily summons to prayer.

From the mosque, five times each day, there comes a reminder to recognize the presence of a Higher Power. It is a constant prompting that all people are spiritual beings.

I wonder how our lives would change if we had an inner reminder of God's love for us—a small bell within that would ring five times a day, instead of the one hour, one Sunday a week reminder?

How wonderful it would be if we stopped to say, "Thank you, God" at dawn, noon, afternoon, sunset and nightfall.

Affirmation: I will recognize God's blessings five times a day.

NAMASTE

August 12

Dreams

"Our dreams can contain messages from God."
-Author

Very often, dreams bring us insights and answers to what is going on in our lives.

Recently, I was troubled by a relationship in which a dear friend of mine was involved. The woman he was dating seemed so unlike him. She appeared unfriendly and totally possessive of this man.

Being the blunt soul that I am, I questioned him about what his love was based on.

I listened attentively as my friend graciously acquiesced to that which was absolutely none of my business by telling me about her childhood and her present life. He then pointed out her numerous good qualities.

When I went to bed that night I asked God, as I always do, to give me instructions through my dreams.

He lovingly answered my request. I dreamt I was in my kitchen with my friend's companion. We were preparing a meal together, laughing and talking. My heart was full and overflowing with love for this woman.

My guidance came through a dream. I guess sometimes God finds it necessary to anesthetize us in order to teach us our lessons—lessons such as non-judgment.

Yay for sleeping and dreaming!

Affirmation: Dreaming is another pathway to understanding.

NAMASTE

August 13
The Power Within

"The power that resides in him is new in nature, and none but he knows what that is which he can do, nor does he know until he has tried."

-Ralph Waldo Emerson

Until I was sixty years old, I had no idea how to usher my passion into this world. I was too busy being the perfect wife and mother, followed by years of playing the go-getter executive assistant.

When I was forced to quit working because of health challenges, I lay in my bed and quietly let the magic of my creative mind catch up with me.

Writing became a passion, something I never knew I could do. Words flowed like a rain-swollen creek. My mind simply would not shut off. As Emerson suggested in the opening quotation, the power within me was new. I simply did not know what I could do until I took the time to try.

Affirmation: I will stop long enough for my passion to find me.

NAMASTE

Beauty

"I have lov'd the principle of beauty in all things . . . ."
-John Keats

Where do you see beauty? Is it in the smile of a newborn? The bloom of a rose? The radiance of the sun? Or, perhaps, you see beauty in everything and everyone you encounter.

"Beauty is in the eye of the beholder" is a well-known adage and it is most certainly true. I may find the paintings of Renoir to be breathtaking, while you might enjoy the works of Picasso.

It doesn't matter what we deem beautiful, what is important is that we recognize the loveliness in our everyday lives, that we breathe in the beauty of ordinary things and, in so doing, nourish our souls.

Affirmation: I see beauty everywhere.

NAMASTE

Seeing God in Grandma

"A loving grandmother is the personification of all of God's creations."
-Author

Grandmothers have always played an important role in family life, and mine was no exception.

As a youngster, I can remember visiting my grandmother in the summer and sleeping on her front porch. Embraced by the dense honeysuckle vines entwined throughout a large, wooden trellis, I would enjoy both privacy and the pleasant, sweet aroma of the flower's delicate yellow-white blooms.

Grandma's house was a haven of security for me. Born in 1936, I was just six years old when our country entered into the Second World War. My dad joined the Navy and, for a time, my mother, sister and I lived with my grandparents.

I remember Grandma's lavender bush next to the driveway and how she would pick a branch from it and place the pungent offshoot into her handbag before getting into the car alongside Grandpa. She always smelled of lavender.

I recall, also, sitting in the huge back yard under the English walnut tree, surrounded by Grandpa's rose bushes and enjoying the delicious aromas wafting from the Wonder Bread Bakery around the corner from their house.

Because my grandparents' home was always overflowing with aunts, uncles and cousins, each morning, Grandma would get up early to bake a chocolate cake and a few dozen oatmeal cookies. She wanted to make sure that no one ever left her house hungry.

I often compare the Beloved to my precious grandmother: the loving security of God's vine-like protection, the lavender-like essence of His grace and the constant feeding of my soul through reading, prayer and meditation—the giving of His heavenly manna.

I will forever remember the goodness and the God-ness that was my grandmother.

Affirmation: I see God in grandmothers everywhere.

NAMASTE

August 16
Walking With God

"Oh! For a closer walk with God."
-Olney Hymns (1779), no. 1,
Walking with God

My life is a song of love, a creation of the Beloved. It is a daily, compassionate walk along a pathway of joyous terrain sprinkled here and there with near-insurmountable obstacles.

Through the years, I will allow the All-Knowing, All-Loving One to take my hand and walk with me, filling me with astounding beauty, tingling excitement and a burning love for life.

Affirmation: I walk this life with a constant knowledge of the presence of God.

NAMASTE

August 17
Giving and Receiving Comfort

"I'm very brave, generally, only today I happen to have a headache."
-Tweedledum

Our journey through life often includes situations that cause us to grab the hand of another in order to keep walking on our path.

Does this mean that we're weak? Absolutely not! It merely means that we're human.

We all have those moments when we need a shoulder to cry on or arms to embrace us in order that we might, once again, find our own balance. Then, when the tides turn, we can be that shoulder and those arms for another.

Affirmation: I can both receive and give comfort.

NAMASTE

August 18

Beauty From Within

"Real beauty is created through a loving soul."
-Author

Have you ever known someone who, in spite of physical appearance, was the most beautiful person you ever met? It wasn't the outer attractiveness that drew you to them, it was the sparkle in their eyes, the smile on their lips and their gentle essence.

We often judge people by their looks. How sad is that?

Looking at a person's soul and not his/her physical appearance will bring a clearer, more beautiful picture of that person.

Affirmation: I look to the soul to find the beauty in everyone I meet.

NAMASTE

Being Peace

"I love tranquil solitude."
-Shelley

"Peace" and "tranquility" are words that, if repeated over and over, almost as a mantra, bring to us the essence of their meaning.

Right now, close your eyes and, with each breath in, repeat, in your mind, the word "peace." Then, with every outgoing breath, say the word "tranquility." Do this until you feel the astounding effects of these two, small words.

This is what I call breathing in the Beloved. It can be done anywhere—at your desk, in the car while waiting for a train to pass, or in your home, resting in your special chair. I do it often on my front porch, listening to the chatter of mocking birds and inhaling the aromas of whatever season it might be.

Lifted from time and space, I breathe in the essence of the Beloved.
Lifted from the chatter of my own mind, I go to that silent place of nothingness.
Lifted from all that is mortal, I connect with All That Is.
And I am more fully alive.
-Author

Affirmation: I take time for peace and tranquility.

NAMASTE

An Indigo Child Named Chanse

*"Grandchildren are the precious gems in the jewel
boxes of every grandparent."*
-Author

Tonight, I sit on my candlelit front porch remembering my day—one of the most magical of my life.

Not only am I back on my feet, but, this week, my adopted grandson's mother is celebrating her birthday, and Chanse asked if Bill and I could help him prepare a special dinner for her.

So at ten o'clock this morning, we picked up our "adorable grandy," and, with some recipes that he had "borrowed" from his mother, we went shopping for her favorite meal.

The afternoon was spent setting the table with great care, preparing the food and making sure that the four other guests, as well as Chanse's mother and dad, would arrive promptly at six.

When everyone had settled in their chairs, at the dining room table, Chanse lit all of the candles, saw to it that each crystal goblet was filled with sparkling cider and that every person was served. Then the party began!

He later told his mother how much he loved his extended family.

What a gem this young man is to us and all who know him—a strong force of Indigo love!

Affirmation: It is in the magical moments of familial love, the building of memories, that my life is nurtured.

NAMASTE

August 21
Buddhist Loving Kindness

"Love alone matters."
-Saint Therese of Lisieux

Recently I have had the privilege of attending a class on metta sutta meditation. Metta, translated from Pali, means "love," or "loving kindness." Sutta, also from Pali, refers to a "discourse" (in this case, phrases) that the Pali canon attributes to the Buddha or one of his disciples.

In this practice, we use traditional loving sutta phrases for ourselves and others.

To start this meditative process, we first close our eyes and repeat several times:

I breathe in love from God (or whatever Higher Power name you prefer.)

I breathe out love to God

Then we choose phrases that attune to our wishes. We first say these phrases for ourselves. The words I chose were:

May I be loving and kind

May I be happy and peaceful

May I be free from mental, physical and emotional suffering

May I be healthy, strong and vibrant

May I always live joyfully with ease

May all sentient beings be at ease

After doing metta sutta for myself, I then do it for:

A loved one

(Example:

    May Bill (my husband) be loving and kind   ·

    May Bill be happy and peaceful

    May Bill be free from mental, physical and emotional suffering

    May Bill be healthy, strong and vibrant

    May Bill always live joyfully with ease

    May all sentient beings be at ease)

A neutral person (such as the mailman or grocery clerk)

A teacher (someone who has taught me either spiritually or educationally)

A difficult person in my life

For every sentient being

Remember, for each person you do metta sutta, you start by breathing in that person's love for you and breathing out your love for him or her.

One morning I stayed in bed for two hours sending out this loving kindness. I sent it first to myself and then to almost everyone I knew. I have continued this each morning.

Oh my! The love that floods my heart is overwhelming!

Try this and see how just saying these simple phrases, or similar phrases of your choice, opens your heart to those for whom you do metta sutta.

Affirmation: I will grow more loving through my metta sutta practice.

NAMASTE

Ecstasy is a Town Called Pismo Beach

"When fortune smiles, embrace her."
-Thomas Fuller

Buying our little place in Pismo Beach was an ecstatic time for me! I remember walking from our house down to the beach. I felt such joy, such freedom! It was one of those rare times of total clarity—clarity of knowing what truly makes me happy.

The experience was one of feeling like I owned the entire town of Pismo. It was being part of something so perfect, so clean, so quaint. The streets were mine, the pier was mine. Even the sand and the waves belonged to only me. It was "Godism." I don't think I have ever felt so alive, so at peace, inside and out.

I can still conjure up those feelings even though my little house is sold—gone. I close my eyes and walk past the magazine store, the salt water taffy shop, Harry's Bar. I look across the street and relive the memories of Brad's, where a shrimp cocktail meant the crunch of celery and a bit hotter than usual, yummy sauce. The corner store where they sold souvenirs and the best cup of cappuccino in town. The long stairway down to the beach where I walked with the seagulls overhead and the waves lapping at my feet. Inspecting the caves carved from the side of the hill. Did I want to live there forever? Oh, yeah!

But the Universe has a way of plucking us up and putting us where we need to be for whatever reason. I am where I am meant to be. And the fond memories sustain me.

Affirmation: With the help of my memories, I can be happy wherever I am. And I can make new memories.

NAMASTE

August 23

Envy

"Envy is the ulcer of the soul."
-Socrates

Envy can take us into the deepest hole of depression. It leaves us feeling depleted and unhappy. Brought on by a feeling of "lack" and "not enough," it is a plague worse than any physical disease.

When we choose to be happy in whatever circumstance we find ourselves, that choice cancels out all envy. Constantly thanking the Beloved for everyone and everything in our lives increases our appreciation for what we already have. It grows us spiritually.

If we truly believe that we are all soul-connected, then when Joe Smith wins the lottery, we, too, win the lottery. When our neighbor buys a brand new car, we can rejoice in his good fortune because it is also our good fortune.

Being happy for others increases our own joyful endorphins.

Try it!

Affirmation: I thank God for all that I have and all that I am.

NAMASTE

Patience

"Adopt the pace of nature; her secret is patience.
Sometimes you don't need the things you "need" to enjoy
the simple things, quiet times, friends, family."
-Amish Proverb

Like a flowing stream, patience glides more freely when we put our full trust in the Beloved. We tend to throw rocks and, even, sometimes, boulders, into our gentle brooks, causing the water to hesitate and seek a path around the blockage.

Many of us, in times of financial or health crises, think we need to do something—anything that will hurry us past the dilemma in order to "get on with life."

I've got news for you! Our crises are part of our lives—a very important part. Those times come along in order to teach us patience, to show us what is truly important—our quiet times with God, our friends and our families.

Adopt the pace of nature, her secret is patience.

Affirmation: I will take winter's bareness, knowing that spring is on its way.

NAMASTE

August 25
Putting Ourselves First

"It is only when we take care of ourselves first that we can,
then, take care of others."
-Author

We have somehow gotten the idea that putting ourselves first is selfish. This is a myth that has kept many of us in bad marriages, made us enablers to our drug or alcohol-addicted children, and kept us from furthering our educations or pursuing the work we love.

We need to listen carefully to flight attendants. They will tell you in their pre-flight instructions that, in case of a loss in cabin pressure, and you are traveling with small children, you are to put the oxygen mask on yourself before assisting others.

Wow! Take care of myself first. There's a fresh concept.

We can care for ourselves by eating healthy food, exercising, sleeping eight hours and having fun enjoying what we love doing the most, both in our work and in our play.

Affirmation: As I fly through life, I will take loving care of myself first.

NAMASTE

August 26
Life Responds to Us

"Life is not happening to us, life is responding to us."
-Rev. Danell Wheeler

Every time we think a thought or speak a word, we are creating our reality, making our existence on this earth either positive or negative—heaven or hell.

Life just naturally responds to every thought we think and every word we utter.

Gossip not about people but about all of the good that is happening in our lives. When we stop gossiping and complaining, we often find that we have absolutely nothing to say. After a while we begin bursting forth with good news and the joy that is in our lives because we have created those things with our positive thoughts and words.

Start each morning by saying, "Today is one of the best days of my life!" and watch it happen!

Affirmation: Today is one of the best days of my life!

NAMASTE

August 27

Ice Cream for the Soul

"Out of the mouth of babes and sucklings thou hast perfected praise."
-Matthew 21:16

Today I would like to share with you a charming story whose author is unknown.

"Last week I took my children to a restaurant. My six-year-old son asked if he could say grace. As we bowed our heads he said, 'God is good. God is great. Thank you for the food, and I would even thank you more if mom gets us ice cream for dessert. And Liberty and justice for all! Amen.'

Along with the laughter from the other customers nearby, I heard a woman remark, 'That's what's wrong with this country. Kids today don't even know how to pray. Asking God for ice-cream! Why, I never!' Hearing this, my son burst into tears and asked me, 'Did I do it wrong? Is God mad at me?' As I held him and assured him that he had done a terrific job and God was certainly not mad at him, an elderly gentleman approached the table. He winked at my son and said, 'I happen to know that God thought that was a great prayer.'

'Really?' my son asked.

'Cross my heart.'

Then in a theatrical whisper he added (indicating the woman whose remark had started this whole thing.) 'Too bad she never asks God for ice cream. A little ice cream is good for the soul sometimes."

Naturally, I bought my kids ice cream at the end of the meal. My son stared at his for a moment and then did something I will remember the rest of my life. He picked up his sundae and without a word walked over and placed it in front of the woman. With a big smile he told her,

'Here, this is for you. Ice cream is good for the soul sometimes, and my soul is good already.'"

Affirmation: Ice cream and love are good for the soul.

NAMASTE

August 28
Quiet Love

"Till I loved I never lived—enough."
-Emily Dickinson

Love flows over me this morning, love as warm and comforting as the sun shining down on my front porch. I feel like a sage—a tribal elder wanting to impart some piece of loving wisdom to the circle that surrounds me. I stare into the imaginary fire burning in the center of our gathering and can't think of a single word to say—can't seem to access my "sageness."

Then I look up and realize that the same, golden sun that cascades over me is pouring on, between and around everyone in the sacred circle. Love, I discover, doesn't always need words. In blessed stillness, it simply flows from one person to the other, proving that we are all soul-and-sunshine-connected.

My thoughts today are simply those of love for you, my readers, as well as for the vast Universe that surrounds us.

Affirmation: Today I move and have my being in love.

NAMASTE

August 29
Sacred Breath

"The heart must pause to breathe."
-Lord Byron

Shakespeare talks of 'summer's ripening breath,' and Wordsworth speaks of "A child that lightly draws its breath." He also said "Poetry is the breath and finer spirit of all knowledge."

"Spiritus," the Latin origin of the word spirit, means "breath." In meditation, we concentrate on our breathing, feeling ourselves become calm and relaxed with each inhale and exhale.

We are most at peace when our minds are centered on Spirit, when we become mindful of our "breaths."

Affirmation: I relax into Infinite Breath.

NAMASTE

August 30
Renewing Warmth

"The sunshine is a glorious birth."
-William Wordsworth

I have been sitting on my front porch for over an hour, and, now, the morning sun sits warm against my cheek.

All thoughts have calmed and I shift my consciousness, allowing me to fully encounter my oneness with the Beloved. The tranquility is all-embracing.

I have been allowed this time of inner stillness and the loving warmth of God's sunshine to replenish my body and restore my soul. Once again, I can create with renewed vigor and emotion that which God has given me to do.

For this and so much more I am truly grateful.

Affirmation: I rest and create—rest and create—rest and create.

NAMASTE

August 31
Divine Potential

"We ignite our lives when we fan the flames of inspiration."
-Author

I am eager to embrace this day, to begin it filled and overflowing with the essence of thanksgiving and joy.

How can I be otherwise, when my life is such an exciting adventure that both inspires and bids me to express the myriad strengths and gifts that God has bestowed upon me?

Silently, I release all sense of limitation. I am filled to overflowing with the knowledge that I can do, be and create everything that the Beloved placed me on this earth to do, be and create.

Affirmation: I will manifest my divine potential.

NAMASTE

September 1
Hearts

"Our first teacher is our heart."
-Cheyenne saying

Our hearts are regarded as the center of thought and emotion. We hear such expressions as, "He has no heart," "take heart," "I've had a change of heart," "Let's get to the heart of the matter," "He is a good person at heart," "She is close to my heart," "Let's have a heart to heart talk," and, "I love you with all of my heart."

As embryos, our first hearing and feeling experience is the beating of our mother's heart. It is common practice that when a baby animal is taken from its mother, a ticking clock is often tucked in its bed to mimic the beating of that loving organ.

Both joy and grief are expressed with our hearts and when we think of God, often we think of that Great Force as the Heart of the Universe.

St. Augustine declared, "O Lord, you have created us for Yourself and our hearts are restless until they rest in Thee." Sitting Bull, a Sioux Indian Chief, once said, "Great Spirit put in your heart certain wishes and plans; in my heart, He put other and different desires."

Remember that your heart's desire is always a message from God. Listen carefully.

Affirmation: I will turn off my mind and listen to my heart.

NAMASTE

September 2

Mother Nature's Glorious Red

"For thee the wonder-working earth puts forth sweet flowers."
-Titus Lucretius Carus

From my front porch, this afternoon, I gaze around at the glorious color red—red roses, hollyhocks, geraniums, hibiscus, and pomegranates dangling from my neighbor's tree. So much exquisite color!

The green background of leaves, bushes, and grass and the cerulean blue overhanging sky add gentle contrast to all of the magnificent reds.

God is the ultimate artist, the creator of Mother Nature's babies. He is the choreographer of the whispering, fluttering dance of leaf and bud, the Majestic Designer of all things red.

Affirmation: I will open my eyes to the beauty of color around me.

NAMASTE

September 3
The Winds Of September

"Poetry is merely the gentle whispering of God."
-Author

As I rest on my front porch this morning with my furry Zen master dozing beside me, I notice the leaves of both the crepe myrtle and the camphor trees fluttering in the frenzied, whipping Santa Ana winds.

I sit quietly and hear a gentle whisper, offering me these words:

I am still and listening,
Not to a learned wise man
But to the rustle of wind-swept leaves.

To the unfolding of purple morning glories
Kissed by the rising sun,
And the gentle cooing of an awakening dove.

I harken to the beat of an egret's wings
As it takes flight and soars,

The Universe is humming with the utterance of life,
And I hear throughout creation
The soft, echoing voice of God.
-Author

Affirmation: I sit still in the morning sunrise and listen to the awakening world.

NAMASTE

September 4

Why Not Just Ask?

"Ask, and it shall be given you . . . ."
-Matthew 7:7

In the past I always thought I had to control my life—my comings and goings. Now I simply ask God for things, for people and for places and they seem to just magically appear.

When I wanted to find a new Spiritual Home—a place where I could recharge my "holy batteries," I explained to Spirit that I didn't really believe in a "God in the box" church and so it was up to Him to find my exact right place. This asking happened on a Saturday morning. The following Wednesday a woman showed up at my Writers' Critique Group and invited me to a spiritual center called "Common Ground"—a place not even four miles from my home.

In a welcoming letter, the minister wrote, "We endeavor to transcend the boxes of religion to reveal the universal concept of kindness, love and compassion." Could the Beloved have sent me to a better place?

My theme here is that you first think about what your needs and your wants are and then ask for them, knowing that they will appear.

Bill and I have been attending Common Ground for a number of years now, and it so perfectly fits our spiritual needs.

I merely asked Spirit for what I wanted and, in turn, it was provided. It's as simple and as miraculous as that!

Affirmation: All I have to do is knowingly ask.

NAMASTE

September 5

Vision

"I will pour out my spirit on all flesh; your sons and your daughters shall prophesy, your old men shall dream dreams, your young men shall see visions."

-Joel 2:28

According to the English writer, Jonathan Swift, "Vision is the art of seeing things invisible."

Often, in meditation, and also during a dream state, we will get a vision of something God wants us to do or be.

Every time I sit down to write, I envision Divine Intelligence inspiring me and creating through me.

We must develop the visionaries that we are, hone the art of seeing that which is not yet in form.

Affirmation: I will be a visionary.

NAMASTE

September 6

Underwhelmed

"Today I choose to be "underwhelmed."
-Author

Again and again we hear people saying, "I am totally overwhelmed!" It usually means they are too busy, bogged down in excesses, or experiencing personal, financial or physical challenges.

These are the times that they need to take a deep breath and rest in the awareness of the Blessed Underwhelmer.

Slow down during this autumn season and watch the changing color of the leaves, knowing that God, in His infinite mercy, will soon allow these dying leaves of burden to float down and fly away on the gentle winds of peace.

Affirmation: "Underwhelmed" is good.

NAMASTE

September 7
Life Doesn't Have to Be One Big Yawn

"Life can be either a giant, boring yawn or an enormous, hearty laugh."
-Author

There is a remarkable woman at our Spiritual Center. We call her Dr. Jean. When she sees you, her emerald eyes sparkle, her warm grin widens and her arms automatically wrap around you in a great bear hug. When Dr. Jean hugs you, you know you've been hugged! She is the Spiritual Center's leader for our "teens," finding projects in the community that need doing, and then she and our teenagers get to work.

Dr. Jean is a must at every party. Her laughter is contagious, her love is depthless and her spirit shines forth like the beacon on a lighthouse.

What does this over sixty-year-old woman do for a living? She counsels deprived and homeless teens and young adults. In her challenging career, Dr. Jean integrates a tough-love approach that carries with it more unconditional love than these young men and women ever dreamed existed.

Her life is an exciting, everyday challenge accompanied by a hearty laugh. Dr. Jean simply does not have time to yawn!

Affirmation: I will choose a hearty laugh over a ho-hum yawn.

NAMASTE

Zeal

"What one has, one ought to use; and whatever he does,
he should do with all his might."
-Cicero

Just as an active volcano bubbles up and overflows, so must our zeal for life!

Loving our lives, being zealous and impassioned, brings on unimaginable, creative energy. It puts a grin on our faces and a spring in our steps.

To be stimulated by life brings us closer to all of humanity and allows us a deeper awareness of all that exists.

Zeal adds flavor to our everyday walk on this earth. Like salting our food, it adds spice to our lives.

Henry David Thoreau said it so beautifully, "If the day and night be such that you greet them with joy, and life emits a fragrance like flowers and sweet-scented herbs, is more elastic, more starry, more immortal—that is your success. All nature is your congratulation, and you have cause momentarily to bless yourself."

RIGHT ON, Henry!

Affirmation: I will live my life with zeal!

NAMASTE

September 9

God's Elegant Bouquet

"Child, you are like a flower, so sweet and pure and fair."
-Heinrich Heine

A fall bouquet could very well contain a variety of flowers in a medley of beautiful, vivid colors: chrysanthemums, those gentle puffs of white, bronze and russet blooms; dahlias, so diverse in their glorious colors, shapes and sizes; stunning asters, with their brightly-hued, daisy-like flowers; and, delphinium, those elegant pink and lavender perennials that rise gracefully above lush, green foliage.

I like to think of myself as one flower in a large bouquet of mankind, enjoying the unique beauty of us all; each one a divine expression of God. Whether I am a velvety chrysanthemum, a glorious dahlia, a stunning aster, or an elegant delphinium, I appreciate my likeness and my difference to all of the others in the bouquet.

Affirmation: I am a single one, yet a oneness with all, in God's beautiful bouquet.

NAMASTE

September 10
Make Your Home Your Own

"Stay, stay at home, my heart, and rest; home-keeping
hearts are happiest."
-Henry Wadsworth Longfellow

Bill and I have created a kitchen in our home that makes me want to dance when I enter it—not necessarily cook, mind you, but dance.

We have decorated it in a retro red-and-white cherry theme—shades of the 40s and 50s. Our floor consists of large black-and-white vinyl squares and we have further "antiqued" up our kitchen with cabinets, trinkets and gadgets of days long gone by. This bright room connects us to our childhoods.

Just as my husband and I have done, may I suggest that you surround yourself with the smells, textures and objects that bring back good memories for you. Carefully choose the things you want to enjoy on a daily basis. Fill your home with those objects that bring "warm fuzzy" feelings to you.

Oh! The timer in the kitchen just went off. The chocolate chip cookies are ready to come out of the oven.

Bill bakes!

I dance!

YES!

Affirmation: I will surround myself with loving memories and chocolate chip cookies.

NAMASTE

September 11
Bringing Forth Our Love

"In this world, hate never yet dispelled hate. Only love dispels hate.
This is the law, ancient and inexhaustible."
-Buddha

The disaster of September 11, 2001, is an event that will live on in my memory forever. Bill and I were at our home in Pismo Beach when the Twin Towers went down.

The phone rang, and my daughter said, "Mom, turn on the television." When the picture came onto the screen, I could not comprehend what flashed before my eyes. How could any pilot so misjudge his flight path?

When I realized what had happened, I bowed my head in grief for those in the towers, for the atrocity of hate that caused this horrendous act, and for the families whose loved ones would not be coming home from work that evening.

In the days following 9/11, we as a nation, shone like the incredible stars that we are. Love avalanched down a mountain of caring with donations of blood, flying of flags from homes and car windows, and notes of sympathy written to the bereaved families.

How many years will it take for us to learn that hate is a disease which can only be cured by a hefty dose of love?

Affirmation: I will hold onto the experience after 9/11 in order to remember the importance of love and all that it means.

NAMASTE

Changing Seasons

"Therefore all seasons shall be sweet to thee."
-Samuel Taylor Coleridge

The final, lingering days of summer have pushed on, leaving room for cool days and a flourish of confetti yellow and amber leaves on the trees.

Change is inevitable, not only in the seasons, but also in our lives. Something in each of us shifts as spring turns to summer and fall to winter. As earth undergoes her own transformation, something deep within us does the same.

Each season, stop and feel—truly feel—the emotions that come up for you.

All of my emotions are connected to my youth and yet they show up year-after-year.

In the autumn, I remember looking forward to the excitement of a new school year; to a bright red pencil box, colorful pumpkins, trick-or-treating and, then, Thanksgiving at Grandma's.

Winters bring with them the memories of quiet times spent indoors, Blondie and Dagwood coloring books, movie star paper dolls, popcorn popped in a wire cage over a crackling fire and the joy of spending Christmas with all of my large, extended family gathered around a huge dining room table.

Spring always carries with it the budding of the over-two-hundred rose bushes that my grandfather tended so lovingly, spirited Easter egg hunts and new, lacy, pastel dresses.

In the summer, I am reminded of the ocean and our playful, annual vacations at Carmel-by-the-Sea.

Each season, I breathe in the essence of those memories, feel the excitement of the then and there as well as the here and now.

Affirmation: I will make each season of my life a joyful experience.

NAMASTE

September 13
The Lost Art of Letter-Writing

"A letter always seemed to me like immortality."
-Emily Dickinson

In this era of e-mailing, twittering and texting, we seem to have forgotten that the very act of jotting a note or writing a letter to someone gives them a communication that becomes part of their history—a bit of the past in your own handwriting.

A letter or a postcard can be kept and savored for years. I have letters in my "Precious Box" written by relatives who, years ago, made their transitions. How wonderful it is to periodically take out these notes and let those loving personalities come alive once again.

Affirmation: I will buy some stationery and post cards and write to my loved ones.

NAMASTE

September 14
Those Popcorn Moments

"When a child laughs, the Universe sings."
-Author

When my children were very young, our Sunday night ritual was to eat popcorn and sliced oranges. The popcorn was always put into a large, blue bowl that had been a wedding gift to my mother and father.

On one such evening, I poured the customary kernels into a pot in which I had melted the usual butter. I placed the lid on the pot and shook it over a lighted burner on the stove. As always, my two eager youngsters stood by my side waiting, excitedly, for the first kernel to pop.

It seems that I had poured an overabundance of kernels into the pan and, as the corn continued to pop, the lid rose higher and higher until popcorn flew out of the pot and around the kitchen like fluffy, shooting fireworks.

My son, who was three at the time, laughed so hard that he fell to the floor while the warm snowflakes of popped corn gathered around his small body.

How many "popcorn moments" can we provide for our children? They are never-forgotten-moments that remain in our memories and our hearts forever.

Affirmation: I will make "popcorn memories" for myself and my children.

NAMASTE

September 15
God's Puzzle

"The idea of separateness is merely an illusion of the human mind."
-Author

How many times have we heard people say, "When I die, I have a million unanswered questions I need to ask God?"

It is difficult for us mortals to understand God's overall plan. It's particularly hard when we go through our dark nights of the soul.

It helps for me to understand that what happens in my life similarly happens to every sentient being. I am merely one piece of God's beautiful puzzle.

When I focus only on me as that single piece, I can't see the whole picture. But, if I stand back and view the entire finished puzzle, it helps me to know that I am a part of God's perfect plan.

Affirmation: I view the completed puzzle and see through the illusion of separateness.

NAMASTE

September 16
Torn Between Two Loves

"Life is a balancing act."
-Author

My love for writing asks that I spend many hours alone in contemplation, prayer and meditation. Oh, those sweet moments of creativity when I listen quietly until the Divine gives me the ingredients for yet another tasty morsel to "cook up" and pass along.

My love for people, however, is equally as strong, begging me to get out there and play, to throw yet another dinner party, to go on an exciting adventure with my friends and family.

During the three years, so far, that it has taken me to write these epistles, I have had to listen very carefully to my Co-Creator; to take orders, so to speak, from my Commanding Officer in order to balance my writing with my social life.

Spending too much time writing often brings with it an agonizing loneliness. That's when I know God wants me "out there" kicking up my heels—experiencing life so that when, once again, I hunker down, I will have another tasty morsel to pass along.

Affirmation: I balance my life.

NAMASTE

September 17
Receive Each Day as a Perfect Gift

"As long as I am on "this side of the dirt" as opposed to "under it," I plan to kick up my heels and live every day to the fullest!"
-Author

We cannot afford to lose even one day of our lives. Each day is a perfect gift waiting to be opened—each minute and hour, a rich, dark chocolate truffle waiting to be savored!

The first thing we can do in the morning is give thanks for the upcoming surprises that await us. Giving thanks each day multiplies the experiences for which we can be thankful; so that by the time our heads hit the pillow at night we've had a bushel-full of fruitful life experiences. It's like going to the mailbox each day, knowing that we've won that day's lottery and the check is in the mail. Or, maybe, picking up the phone and the voice on the other end says, "Your name has been drawn, and you've won a trip to the Caribbean."

Life is to be lived with only positive expectations—a glorious dance with the Beloved! Make it just that and you will not have wasted one precious day!

Affirmation: I live every day to the fullest.

NAMASTE

September 18
We Are All Eternally Fabulous

"Realizing that she is fabulous at any age is a
woman's finest beauty product."
-Author

Our family is in the midst of planning a birthday party for a daughter who came into my life when she was thirteen-years-old. In six days, Dana will be reaching the mid-century mark. My daughter, Debbie, has themed the party "Fabulous at Fifty". She has left no space in her home and back yard undecorated or "unglittered." It will be a sparkling night of fun and fantasy.

Dana is fabulous at fifty, and she will be at seventy, ninety and one hundred as well.

When we realize that we are a soul living in a body, the age of that body is nothing compared to the agelessness of our souls.

We must stop thinking of ourselves as "old" and become cognizant of the fact that we are, above all else, "eternal."

Affirmation: I see myself as fabulous at every age.

NAMASTE

September 19
What Does it Mean to Be Alive?

"When I'm deep awake, I truly appreciate the magic of existence."
-Tim Freke
How Long is Now?

What is our understanding of what it means to be alive? Are we sleep-walking through life, unaware of what's going on around us, getting up in the morning and then going to bed at night with only a profound emptiness in between?

The Master of Wonder bids us to revel in our senses, to smell, taste, touch and hear all of the marvelous delights of God's creative gifts. We are living in a stomping ground of epiphanies, a kingdom of miracles. Hunt them! Find them! Dig them up!

Each morning know what Henry Wadsworth Longfellow knew when he said,

"Life is real! Life is earnest!"

Affirmation: I experience a deep, inspiring understanding of what it is to be alive.

NAMASTE

September 20
First Rain

"The thirsty earth soaks up the rain,
And drinks, and gapes for drink again.
The plants suck in the earth, and are
With constant drinking fresh and fair."
Abraham Cowley

I look outside this morning at diffused light filtering through the trees from a sky somber with clouds. A gentle, quiet rain, not even enough to dimple the surface of our pond, falls delicately, bringing with it relief from the dryness of the smothering, summer heat.

With the onset of first-rain, grass, trees and bushes shine and dance, their leaves and blades inflated with moisture. New life and spirited vigor seem apparent in every living thing.

I move quietly out the door and onto my front porch to inhale deeply the delicate fragrance of the dampened soil and to watch the tiny wrens chattering happily as they flap their silken wings, flying from tree to tree in gay abandon, playing in God's gentle sprinkler.

Life has turned another corner, a lovely, agile shift from summer to autumn.

The rain has come!

Affirmation: The rains come down, all nature sings.

NAMASTE

September 21
International Day of Peace

"The God of Victory is said to be one-handed, but
peace gives victory to both sides."
-Ralph Waldo Emerson

As I write this vignette, it is 9:30 at night and my husband and I have just returned from an International Day of Peace celebration sponsored by our town's Interfaith Association.

This day, September 21, is the day that the United Nation's sponsors "The International Day of Peace." It was established in 1981 as an opportunity for individuals, organizations and nations to encourage peace.

The resolution states: "Peace Day should be devoted to commemorating and strengthening the ideals of peace both within and among all nations and peoples . . . . This day will serve as a reminder to all peoples that . . . . our permanent commitment, above all interests or differences of any kind, is to peace."

During this evening's sacred celebration, we repeated prayers together as a group of people from every faith. Among those prayers for peace were: a Jewish prayer, a Baha'i prayer, a Tibetan prayer, a Muslim prayer, a Buddhist prayer, a Hindu prayer, and a Christian prayer.

One of the most beautiful was a Taoist prayer, and I share that with you now.

If there is to be peace in the world,
There must be peace in the nations.
If there is to be peace in the nations,
There must be peace in the cities.
If there is to be peace in the cities,
There must be peace between neighbors.
If there is to be peace between neighbors,
There must be peace in the home.
If there is to be peace in the home,
There must be peace in the heart.

-Lao Tse

Affirmation: I allow the peace in my heart to spread throughout the world.

NAMASTE

Positive Thoughts Create a Positive Life

"There was never anything that did not proceed from thought."
-Ralph Waldo Emerson

I love those words of Emerson! I love the pictures in my mind that they inspire! Knowing that my thoughts create my desires will keep my thinking positive. Reminding myself that I am one with the Beloved opens my soul to that which is eager to express Itself through me. I plant the seed of goodness, and that seed grows, over time, blossoming into that which I desire.

We need to say "EXCUSE ME?" to the negative thoughts that pop into our mind and quickly change them to a higher, more positive frequency. Oh, that doesn't mean we won't react to our feelings—we need to express grief, anger and hurt at the appropriate times; however, if we can accept these feelings and even embrace them, we can work through them much faster—much gentler. Then we can get back to our "warm fuzzies."

Plant a warm, positive thought in your mind this morning and repeat it, like a mantra, all day. Remember to use enthusiasm and joy in your thought, and then see what happens. If a negative thought inches in, just say, "EXCUSE ME?" and let it go.

This exercise will fine-tune your soul so that you can become the instrument through which life flows—the Stradivarius that sings.

Affirmation: Today I think positive thoughts.

NAMASTE

Every Day—A New Adventure

"New things are made familiar, and familiar things are made new."
-Samuel Johnson

Autumn is my favorite season. The heat is waning, the air is damp, and the cool breeze begs me to walk with it.

This morning, sitting on our front porch, Punkie and I look around us and see the crystals of autumn—leaves turning jasper red, calcite yellow and orange. Even Punkie wears these fall colors. Her coat is deep-brown and pumpkin-hued. Goethe put it so beautifully when he said, "Nature is the living, visible garment of God."

Closing my eyes, I can feel God as near to me as my next breath. I embrace The Presence and know that, like the season, Spirit will bring about new adventures for me. After all, isn't that what life is all about, a constant series of adventures?

I like to think of my life in terms of magical encounters. From arising in the morning, and all throughout the day, I have the opportunity to sit at my imaginary spinning wheel, turning wool into yarn, and, with that yarn, crocheting a whimsical pattern that suits me perfectly.

For all of us, whether that pattern is standing side-by-side with a co-worker, mothering our children, planting a garden of sweet-smelling lavender or sharing the day with others in our assisted-living compounds, we have the opportunity to create our each-day's new adventure exactly as we want it to be.

Affirmation: Today, with the Beloved, I co-create a magical adventure.

NAMASTE

September 24
Windmills of Love

"When we love, we utilize the strongest power in the universe."
-Rev. Danell Wheeler

How would our lives look and feel if, like windmills, following the direction of the wind, we let our souls be guided by the action of the metaphorical winds of love?

Our lives would be so peaceful if we "rotated" solely under the force of the gentle passing of a stream of pure, unconditional love.

Affirmation: I am a windmill, utilizing the strongest power in the universe—LOVE.

NAMASTE

September 25
Moving Mountains

"When sleeping women wake, mountains move."
-Chinese Proverb

Those who carry the feminine traits of love, intuition and kindness are asked, now, more than at any other time, to move mountains—mountains of intolerance, of anger, of unforgiveness and of hatred.

As women, let us wake up and strive to build a better world for our offspring—to be the love, kindness and intuitive souls that the Divine Feminine created us to be.

Affirmation: I will diligently move one mountain at a time.

NAMASTE

Earthdance

"Let us dance to the rhythm of peace."
-Author

September is definitely the month for celebrating peace. On September 21, we recognized the "International Day of Peace," and today we celebrate "Earthdance."

This celebration was originated in 1996 by artist/musician, Chris Dekker, to unite the world through dance and music. Today, it is an event encompassing 360 locations in 60 countries.

Represented in this world event are the musical genres of jazz, conscious hip-hop, folk and many other expressions of dance.

The meaningful moment of each Earthdance celebration is when, exactly at 4:00 P.M. Pacific Daylight Time, every event around the world plays the "Prayer for Peace" track. Below are the words to this memorable prayer:

"We are one global family—all colors, all races—one world united. We dance for peace and the healing of our planet Earth. Peace for all nations. Peace for all communities and peace within ourselves. As we join all dance floors across the world, let us connect heart to heart. Through our diversity we recognize unity. Through our compassion we recognize peace. Our love is the power to transform our world. Let us send it out NOW."

So let's all join in this Earthdance celebration. Turn on your iPods and boogie, waltz, hip-hop or tango through your house, dancing for peace!

Affirmation: My heart sings as I dance for peace.

NAMASTE

September 27

Life

"But if the while I think on thee, dear friend, all losses are
restor'd and sorrows end."
-William Shakespeare

Our lives are sometimes overcome with a great loss. Whether it is the loss of a job, a home, or a relationship, we need to release the heaviness of the burden—let it go. Even without these physical things, our life does go on.

A loss is merely the sign of temporal life, reminding us to appreciate the good that we have right now.

And, through it all, Spirit just might supply us with even greater blessings than we have ever known.

Affirmation: I let go of a sense of loss in order to gain what God has next.

NAMASTE

September 28
The Attunement of God

"Like an elegant Steinway, our lives need continuous tuning."
-Author

When the spinet and the spirit of our lives are tuned properly, we can then enjoy the melodies of our souls.

It is when we are attuned to the Infinite Composer that we allow Him to create the music and lyrics that make up the harmony and cadence of our everyday lives.

How breathtaking the sound of a Chopin nocturne when played on a well-tuned piano and how equally delightful a life lovingly attuned to the Infinite Maestro.

Affirmation: Through prayer and meditation, I am endlessly tuned by the Melodious One.

NAMASTE

September 29

Walking

"Solvitur ambulando—It is solved walking."

So many times when I have been confronted with a problem, a bit of bad news or writer's block, I simply lace up my shoes and go for a walk.

Out in the fresh air my head clears, tears of healing are many times released and, after a while, my balance and clarity return.

Get those tennies out in times of stress and, after a long walk, you'll be shouting, "Hi, life! I'm back!"

Affirmation: A long walk sends me home more alive than when I left.

NAMASTE

Tune Out

"To what are we attaching our vibrations?"
-Author

Whenever we turn on the television news channels, we expose ourselves to mostly negativity. I'm getting so I press the "mute button" until the weather person steps up. I am only interested in whether or not I'll need my umbrella when I go shopping this afternoon.

It makes me want to call the station and ask, "Hey, what exciting and awesomely wonderful thing happened today!?" Then see if they'll send out their scurrying TV news vans to find out.

In his book, Your Ultimate calling, Wayne Dyer says, ". . .refuse to be a vibrational match to anything uninspiring."

Affirmation: I look for the good news.

NAMASTE

October 1

The Three Graces

"Like the Three Graces, we, as women, are all symbols
of charm, beauty and joy."
-Author

I have always been fascinated by the statue of The Three Graces. They are usually depicted not as individuals but together as a trinity. They are representations of charm, beauty and joy—a symbol of compassion and benevolence.

In Greek mythology, The Three Graces were thought to be the daughters of the god, Zeus and the nymph, Eurynome. The Graces were named Aglaia (Splendor,) Euphosyne (Mirth,) and Thalia (Good Cheer.)

The three officiated over social events, bringing joy to Gods and mortals alike. They sang to the gods on Mount Olympus and danced to the music that the god Apollo played on his lyre.

Like the muses, they are thought to bestow upon artists and writers the ability to spawn beautiful works of art.

Affirmation: I, like The Three Graces, exude compassion and benevolence.

NAMASTE

October 2

Becoming Who We Really Are

"If I try to be like him, who will be like me?"
-Yiddish proverb

When I was in my teens, I would be Doris Day for a couple of weeks, singing my heart out and coyly batting my eyelashes at every boy in my class. Then, for a time, I would become Betty Davis, curtly issuing orders in a clipped, wide-eyed manner to anyone within hearing distance. Never knowing what starlet they might wake up to find living in their home, I'm sure my family was extremely thankful when I finally passed through my Hollywood impersonation stage.

Later, I tried mimicking different people that I admired, but they weren't me either. It took years of experimenting with different personalities before I quit looking outward and focused inward to discover the real me.

What I know now about myself is that I am a deeply feeling woman, one who loves unconditionally, who strives to take nothing personally, and utilizes gentle nonattachment. I don't know what else I might uncover, but I do know that with deep introspection and interaction with others, I can discover more of the real me.

Matthew Arnold said, "Resolve to be yourself; and know that he who finds himself, loses his misery."

Affirmation: I will discover the real me.

NAMASTE

October 3

Manifesting the Presence of God

"We manifest God by loving others."
-Author

How can we best manifest the presence of God? That seems to me like a very large assignment, and yet it is so simple.

The Gospel of John (15:12) says, "This is my commandment, that ye love one another as I have loved you."

Unconditional love is the perfect way to model ourselves after God. This kind of love opens us to a pureness of mind that refuses to judge, refuses to take personally anything anyone says about us or to us, and gives us the impetus to live day-by-day fully in the present.

When we love ourselves and others as God loves us, there is nothing we can't be or do. It allows us forgiveness on so many levels and opens us to a life of gratitude and service.

Affirmation: I will model the presence of God through my unconditional love.

NAMASTE

October 4
A Marvelous Miracle

"The age of miracles is forever here!
-Thomas Carlyle

When my dear friend, Claudia, died last January, her daughter, Kathy, invited "the family" to have dinner before the funeral. Nine of us sat together around a table in a private dining room at a nearby restaurant. We talked in hushed tones about the one we had just lost.

Kathy has a step-daughter, Jennifer, with whom she is very close. During the dinner, Jennifer's husband, Ryan, stood and tapped a spoon against his water glass, silencing the room. Then he said, "Tonight we will celebrate the going home of Gram, but, as we all know, life flows in a continuing cycle. Jennifer and I would like to announce the coming of another soul to this earth—we're pregnant!"

Shouts of congratulations and tears so recently flowing in sorrow sprang forth in joy.

When Claudia made her transition, her favorite song, *Somewhere Over The Rainbow*, was softly playing in the background. A few days after the funeral, Kathy and Jennifer were at a local department store, browsing in the baby section. Across the aisle, there was a wall where you could press a button and select a CD. No one was near that wall, yet, out of nowhere, the system started playing *Somewhere Over The Rainbow*. My phone rang immediately after this happened and both Kathy and Jennifer said, through their tears, "Aunt Molly, guess what just happened?"

I firmly believe, through this miracle, that Claudia let Kathy and Jennifer know she was aware of the upcoming birth.

Affirmation: I open my heart, my soul, my eyes and my ears to the miracles around me.

NAMASTE

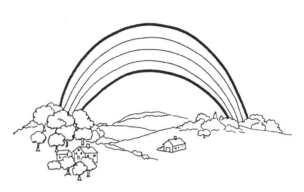

We Can Fly

"I'll teach you to jump on the wind's back, and away we go."
-James Barry

Like Peter Pan, we can all fly. I'm talking about that over-the-moon, metaphorical flight into the unknown.

My favorite dreams are those of flying. In these dreams, I'm free to soar above the earth, feeling the cool breeze on my face, my body supported by the motion of invisible wings.

Twice before in this book, I have shared the metaphor of flying because, to me, just the thought of soaring into the air lifts, not only my body, but my very soul.

Stretch your wings and your mind and experience the uplifting transformation of a flight into the unknown—into the Universe within you.

James Barry wrote, "So come with me, where dreams are born, and time is never planned. Just think of happy things, and your heart will fly on wings, forever, in Never Never Land."

Affirmation: I close my eyes and fly into the sacred unknown.

NAMASTE

October 6
Money, Money, Money

"Focus constantly on your abundance."
-Author

There are two ways we seem to view money. Let me show you in song titles what they are: *Pennies From Heaven,* or *Buddy, Can You Spare a Dime?*

Our attitude about our prosperity falls under the category of, "What we think becomes our reality."

What is money? It's a medium of exchange. It buys us material possessions and services. That's it, folks!

Why do we give the "almighty dollar" so much power, when the Almighty gives us all the love, all the joy, all the blessings, and, yes, all the money we feel we deserve?

Begin today having an attitude of gratitude and there will come forth more and more for which you can be thankful.

Affirmation: I give thanks for all I have, all I give, and all that I receive.

NAMASTE

October 7
Gardening

"He who plants a garden, plants happiness."
-Chinese proverb

I spent this morning in my garden, planting chrysanthemums, zinnias, marigolds and dahlias.

As I dug into the rich soil, preparing a new home for God's burgeoning blooms, the act itself became a ritual of welcoming these flowers into my family.

In the 1800s, Celia Thaxter wrote, "As I work among my flowers, I find myself talking to them, reasoning and remonstrating with them, and adoring them as if they were human beings. Much laughter I provoke among my friends by so doing, but that is of no consequence. We are on good terms, my flowers and I!"

Tonight, as I sit in my sanctuary with my aching muscles, I also remember what Charles Dudley Warner wrote, "What a man needs in gardening is a cast-iron back with a hinge on it."

Affirmation: Today I will give a new home to a variety of autumn flowers.

NAMASTE

October 8
Kuan Yin

"Within every woman lies the spirit of Kuan Yin."
-Author

Outside in my rose garden, there sits a large, regal, stone figure of Kuan Yin. I also have a smaller version in my living room where I have placed a white orchid towering over her like a protective umbrella.

There lies within me a certain fascination for this mother figure. I often stand before her, gathering her strength and security.

Kuan Yin's story is all about love. Just as Mary is the beloved mother for the Catholic faith, so Kwan Yin is the mother figure of the Buddhist faith.

According to Chinese legend, Kuan Yin, when entering heaven, heard a cry of suffering coming from the world beneath her and paused in pity for the weeping. Hence her name: "Kuan (Shih) Yin," (one who notices and hears the cry, or prayers of the world.)

At one time, Kuan Yin was symbolized as a male figure, but in the T'ang Dynasty and Five Dynasties, we find her represented as a woman and has been so since that time.

In whatever Buddhist temple you may be, there is nearly always a chapel for Kuan Yin. She is the patron goddess of mothers, she protects the distressed and at any cry of misery, she hears the voice and removes the sorrow.

She is the model of Chinese beauty, and to say a lady or a little girl is a "Kuan Yin," is the highest compliment that can be paid to elegance and beauty.

Affirmation: Like Kuan Yin, I am finesse, charm and love.

NAMASTE

October 9
Clouds

"You must not blame me if I talk to the clouds."
-Henry David Thoreau

Gazing up at the sky from my front porch this morning, it looks as though the angels had a food fight and tossed mounds of fluffy mashed potatoes all throughout the heavens.

The dark clouds of last night that poured down angry, torrential rains have disappeared, being replaced by their soft, billowy counterparts.

How very much the differing clouds from last night to this morning mimic our ever-changing moods. Our emotions can, one day, be dark and dreary and, the next, be fleecy and light like the mashed potato clouds.

Today's mood? Please pass the gravy!

Affirmation: I accept both the dark and the light clouds of my emotions.

NAMASTE

October 10
Walking on This Earth

"The miracle is not to fly in the air, or to walk on the water,
but to walk on the earth."
-Chinese proverb

When I was in therapy in the 70s, my counselor had me play a game called, "I am aware of." When I looked at someone, I would silently say those words. It made me fully aware of that person's presence. When I took a walk, I would repeat, "I am aware of," and the whole world opened up for me. The natural world around me became more vivid and I was overwhelmed with gratitude for just being alive.

The stars, the moon, the birds, and all flora and fauna are waiting for us to appreciate and love them. As we walk, let us occasionally stop and savor the beauty around us.

Affirmation: I treasure this journey called life.

NAMASTE

October 11
Invictus

"I am the master of my fate.
I am the captain of my soul."
-William Ernest Henley

Nobel Peace Prize winner, Nelson Mandela, while incarcerated on Robben Island for eighteen of his twenty-seven years of confinement, recited the poem "Invictus" to his fellow inmates, giving them the strength and the hope to live.

The poem "Invictus" was written in 1875 by William Ernest Henley as a demonstration of his resilience after his foot had been amputated due to tubercular infection.

This passionate poem is a favorite of mine and I share it with you now:

Out of the night that covers me,
Black as the Pit from pole to pole,
I thank whatever gods may be
For my unconquerable soul.

In the fell clutch of circumstance
I have not winced nor cried aloud.
Under the bludgeonings of chance
My head is bloody, but unbowed.

Beyond this place of wrath and tears
Looms but the horror of the shade,
And yet the menace of the years
Finds, and shall find, me unafraid.

It matters not how strait the gate,
How charged with punishments the scroll.
I am the master of my fate.
I am the captain of my soul.

Affirmation: I am truly the master of my fate and the captain of my soul.

NAMASTE

October 12
The Angel Within

"Hey, there's an angel in me!"
-Nancy Nisonger

We normally think of angels as being "out there," flying around somewhere. When we see them depicted in paintings, they're usually hovering around a person or flocked together in a circle.

We think of these winged cherubs as inhabitants of heaven, guardian angels who show up to comfort us in our times of sorrow or saving us from harm.

Angels are all of this and more.

Hebrews 13:2 says, "Do not neglect to show hospitality to strangers for thereby some have entertained angels unawares."

We all possess the qualities of angels—love, kindness, grace, devotion and compassion.

Angel Dust
> For every loving smile you passed on
> For every embracing hug
> For everyone you touched
> For every kindness you gave freely
> Did you ever stop to think . . . .?
> Hey! There's an angel in me!
> > -Nancy Nisonger

Affirmation: Today I will be an angel to someone in need.

NAMASTE

October 13
Powerful Change

"Change can either strengthen us or bring us down—our choice."
-Author

Change will either fill our sails with the winds of growth or stop us dead in a sea of fear.

We can allow a major change to shut down our lives or use it to strengthen us spiritually and emotionally.

When our plans are altered, we need to ask ourselves, "What is the lesson in this?" Then be very still and listen.

It is when we stop resisting change and simply flow with it that we will find our inner peace.

Affirmation: I will love my life even in the midst of change.

NAMASTE

October 14
Releasing the Coins of Hurt

"Release the past and you will be free to live."
-Author

In the movie, *The King's Speech*, the Duke of York, later to become King George VI, made a wager with his speech therapist. When the Duke lost the wager, he pulled from his pocket, a coin with the picture of his father, King George V on it. It was intimated in the movie that King George V had not always been kind to his son, teasing him about his speech impediment—making him feel "less than."

The speech therapist suggested that "Bertie," as he called the Duke, get rid of all of the coins that had the King's picture on them. "Why do you want to carry your father in your pocket?" he asked.

Do you, like the Duke of York, have painful memories that you carry around in the pocket of your mind?

Let go of those childhood issues that plague you. If necessary, contact a therapist or a friend to help you free yourself from these memories. Try repeating these words, "I lovingly release the past. I am at peace."

Affirmation: I remove all the coins of hurt from my pocket.

NAMASTE

October 15

Who Am I?

"Who do I think I am anyway?"
-Graffiti on a wall in New York

When you are born, you come into a scene that has already been scripted for you by other family members. You're often given a role, such as "black sheep," "little princess," "stupid," or, maybe, "who the hell do you think you are?"

As a child you naturally took the script and acted out the role assigned to you. Then, you grew older and moved off the stage of your birth and onto your own stage, giving you the opportunity to write your own script and the role you wished to play. You could ask yourself, "Who am I?" and answer that question any way you chose.

If you have not yet edited your script and your role, then may I suggest that you picture yourself as a piece of clay and begin to remold your thoughts and your perceptions of yourself. Know that you are a loving, perfect child of the Beloved and become your revised, authentic self.

Affirmation: Today I will edit out the negative in my script.

NAMASTE

October 16

Does It Matter What Others Think?

"If you feel as if your life is a seesaw, perhaps you are depending on another person for your ups and downs."
-Anonymous

Don't allow your self-esteem to be challenged by what other people think or say. After all, whose validation is more important than your own?

We err when we assume that outsiders know better than we do what is right for us.

Listen to that Inner Counsel and you will be listening to the "Larger You."

Affirmation: I trust my own positive validation.

NAMASTE

October 17

Dreams

"I watched the eve
Draw down her shades
With a sweet, delicious sigh.
On to slumber, on to dream
In the velvet arms of night."
-Arlene Hughes

When you lay your head on the pillow tonight, ask the Great Dreamer to speak to you in your dreams. I often ask for ideas to enhance my writing or to solve a problem.

While in college, my first husband would often wake in the middle of the night and race to his drawing board with an answer to a difficult assignment.

For a few nights, before you go to sleep, ask the questions that you want answered in your dreams. Keep a pad and pencil next to your bed, and, first thing in the morning, jot down your dreams before you forget them.

John Keats wrote, "Was it a vision, or a waking dream? Fled is that music: Do I wake or sleep?"

Sweet Dreams!

Affirmation: In my dreams I find the answers.

NAMASTE

October 18
Take Off That Suit of Armor

"I am ashamed of these tears. And yet at the extreme of my misfortune
I am ashamed not to shed them."
-Euripides

Our feelings are part of what makes us human. We must not be ashamed of them.

When we numb ourselves, we internalize both our positive and our negative feelings. Why deny them their expression?

I have known people who walk around stiffly, never allowing their emotions to surface. Someone once said to me, "Don't ever expect me to get excited."

OUCH!

Be grateful for your feelings because it is very difficult to hug a suit of armor.

Affirmation: I am not afraid to cry, laugh or dance!

NAMASTE

October 19
What is Holding You Back From Your Passion?

"Always do what you are afraid to do."
-Ralph Waldo Emerson

When I started writing this book, I was fearful that I wasn't up to the challenge. Now that I am near the finish, I am scared that I will run out of words.

Why do we tremble inside when we hop out of our comfort zones into the unknown? Do we panic, thinking that we are not adequate for the job? Perhaps, we are frightened of success. Either way, we stop ourselves from expressing our life's passion.

How are you holding yourself back? How long will it be before you start living your divine potential?

Follow your bliss and see what happens.

Affirmation: Today I will step out of my comfort zone and live my passion.

NAMASTE

October 20
Balance Your Life

"The really efficient laborer will be found not to crowd his day with
work, but will saunter to his task surrounded by a
wide halo of ease and leisure."
-Henry David Thoreau

How many of us balance our lives?

It seems our tendency is to escape the exuberance of living by burying ourselves in our jobs.

One of the first questions people ask upon meeting a new acquaintance is, "What do you do for a living?" I am often tempted to simply smile and answer, "I breathe. It keeps me joyfully existing."

The Chinese word for "busy" is made up of two characters: "heart" and "killing." When we become obsessed with our work, our lives become a race where the finish line is the flat line on a hospital heart monitor.

Slow down.

Smell the roses.

Live!

Affirmation: I will slow down.

NAMASTE

-336-

October 21
Solitude

"How sweet, how passing sweet, is solitude!"
-William Cowper

There is a peaceful solitude breathing itself about me this morning. I take its essence; hear its soft utterance as it whispers to me of a languid day and a lingering night of blessed communion with my Creator.

And so it is.

Affirmation: I will spend this day in peaceful solitude.

NAMASTE

October 22

Enjoying God

"Just these two words He spoke changed my life, "Enjoy Me."
-St. Teresa of Avila

What a lovely invitation from God! In this bidding, the Beloved invites us to open ourselves to His unconditional love. To enjoy all of the rich gifts that He offers us: the song of a bird; the taste of ice cream; the delicate aroma of a honeysuckle bush; the touch of a lover; the strains of a concerto.

God's invitation to "Enjoy Me" is so vast. All we have to do is open our eyes and our ears to the multitude of amazing gifts He has placed on this earth for our pleasure and delight.

St. Francis of Assisi wrote, "Dear God, please reveal to us your sublime beauty that is everywhere, everywhere, everywhere . . . ."

Affirmation: Today, I will enjoy God.

NAMASTE

October 23
Impromptu Insanity

"I am, so often, a victim of insanity over logic."
-Author

Set the table, cook up a great feast and invite the world over for a celebration of life!

That's exactly what Bill and I did last Sunday. We invited ten people to join us for dinner after our morning worship service.

There was only one problem. All we had at home to eat was a crock pot of homemade soup.

Sooooo, we left our Spiritual Center before anyone else and sped to the nearest grocery store, laughing all the way at our spur-of-the-moment madness.

Inside the store, we grabbed a cart and raced through the aisles. Our gimpy basket clunked its uneven wheel-thumping song as we tossed into it three already-roasted chickens, greens for a salad, goodies from the deli, rolls and desserts.

We plowed through the check-out line, ran to the car, tossed everything into the back seat and raced home, Indy-500-style, beating everyone else by mere minutes.

Our friends dug in, making salads, setting the table and simply enjoying the companionship and the love of being together.

Dancing among friends to a melody of spontaneity and joy is to taste a bit of heaven (and a bit of insanity) here on earth.

Affirmation: Today I will be spontaneous.

NAMASTE

Love 101

"The light of Spirit filters softly through the leaves of the universe."
-Zach McLaughlin

Today, our high school students encounter on-campus challenges that only strong and resilient teenagers can survive. Not only the campus shootings that have occurred in recent years, but also the fights that break out on a regular basis and the online and face-to-face bullying, lead me to believe that another class added to the high school curriculum might be entitled Love 101.

Zach McLaughlin, a young high school student of 16, came to our spiritual center for the first time two years ago. He and his family were looking for a place where they could feel free to express their own Divine Nature.

In the eloquent poem below, Zach writes about what the spiritual center means to him:

Through the Ferns
> In a place of darkness,
> Through the ferns I pass,
> Into the light of unity,
> Into a place of power,
> Onto Common Ground.
>
> In this place,
> Through the ferns,
> I may show my true self
> The mask of society
> Is lifted from my face.

The light of Spirit filters softly
Through the leaves of the universe.

In this place,
I walk slowly, reverently, exploring
A new-found world of light and colors.
I find that my eyes
Were closed to the beauty of the world.

As the light fades,
And my mask forms again,
The darkness is not as dark,
And my eyes remain open,
To the beauty around me.

Affirmation: My darkness is lightened by the presence of God's essence.

NAMASTE

October 25
Detachment

"Disconnect and know."
-Author

Sometimes we need to disconnect ourselves from a problem or a direction in which our life is heading.

At times, maybe a void is necessary in order to tune into the All Knowing.

We must be willing to empty ourselves. For once in our lives, perhaps it would be best to not know in order to know the possibilities that the Beloved can offer.

Often, God gives us more options than we ever dreamed existed if we but disconnect and listen.

Affirmation: I will disconnect and listen.

NAMASTE

October 26

My Prayer

"I open to that all-powerful oneness with God."
-Author

Peace wraps around me tonight like cradling arms. I am content just to "be."

Spirit lingers inside of me. Lives as that Spark Within—that Spark that grows into flames of love at the recognition of Its powerful presence.

For the rest of my days, fill me with You. Show me the You that is me—the truth of who I am.

Take my feet, my hands, my very being, and let them be Yours.

Give me the knowledge of who You are. Breathe Your breath through me.

Affirmation: I am one with God.

NAMASTE

Perseverance

"Give us grace and strength to forbear and to persevere."
-Robert Louis Stevenson

We have a tendency to want our dreams to come true without the time and effort that it takes to make them materialize.

In the writing of this work, I thought a 365-day-book would take one year to complete.

Who was I kidding?

It took me ten years to complete my first novel—ten tedious years of editing and rewrites. *Margo* is now published and my dream has become a reality.

When we can be patient and persevere, our dreams truly do come true.

Never give up!

Affirmation: I will persevere!

NAMASTE

October 28
Walking Your Talk

"What you are stands over you the while, and thunders so that I cannot hear what you say to the contrary."
-Ralph Waldo Emerson

My father's mantra was, "Do as I say, not as I do." As a child, I used to think, but never dared reply, "Why don't you do what is right so you don't have to say those stupid words?"

I have a friend whose father was a minister, preaching love and goodness from the pulpit and then going home after Sunday morning service to beat his family.

Double meanings only confuse our kids. Sure, we all make mistakes, and our children know that. But what they want to see and emulate is a parent who lives a life that matches his/her words.

When you live your truth, the only thunder your children will hear is the noise of a rainy-day storm.

Affirmation: My actions match my words.

NAMASTE

Who or What is God to You?

"They say that God is everywhere, and yet we always think of Him as somewhat of a recluse."
-Emily Dickinson

It is not at all unusual that the great poet, Emily Dickinson, thought of her God as a recluse. She herself was a person who shied away from the public—an agoraphobic who, seldom, if ever, left her home.

We all tend to put God into a context that we can understand. For instance, my Beloved loves to throw a dinner party every chance She gets.

My opinion is that God is in everything and everyone. Spirit is vast, immense and limitless!

Buckminster Fuller said, "God is a verb, not a noun, proper or improper."

Saint Teresa of Avila wrote, "The feeling remains that God is on the journey, too."

And, I love what Vincent Van Gogh said, "But I always think that the best way to know God is to love many things."

Who is God to you?

Affirmation: I open my eyes and see God in my own way.

NAMASTE

October 30
You Are Alive For a Reason

"There is clearly a purpose for our being here at this time in history."
-Author

Do you ever wonder why God chose to bring you to this earth at this time?

Perhaps you have lived past lives and, possibly, you will have future incarnations. But, for whatever reason, you were placed on this earth in this century.

Ask yourself and the Beloved, "Why am I here? What is my mission?"

There is definitely a purpose for your existence at this time in history. Find that purpose, embrace it, fulfill it.

Your mission could very well be to simply love, deeply, sincerely and unconditionally. When we love in that powerful way, our love ripples out to our families, our cities, our states and, even to other nations. What better purpose is there than that in this time of international turmoil?

Affirmation: I will discover the reason why I am here at this particular time and place.

NAMASTE

October 31

Trick-Or-Treat

"What beck'ning ghost, along the moonlight shade, invites my steps,
and points to yonder glade?"
-Alexander Pope

It's Halloween, the time for make-believe, for trick-or-treat, for concocting gooey, sticky popcorn balls, for listening to things that go bump in the night!

Tonight we can be anything we want—a witch, a goblin or, perhaps, a fairy princess.

Why not throw a last-minute Halloween party? Ask everyone you invite to bring their favorite sweet or snack to share, and then play a silly game of Balderdash.

Now-and-then, you might be interrupted by a visiting ghoul at your front door. Just let that be part of the evening's entertainment.

Happy Halloween!

Affirmation: Tonight I'll be a kid again.

NAMASTE

November 1

Devotion

"Devotion is simply the promptitude, fervor, affection and
agility which we have in service of God."
-St. Francis de Sales

There are so many ways of showing our devotion to the Beloved. Catholics make the gentle sign of the cross; other Christian faiths bow their heads and some even fold their hands in prayer; Native Americans dance; Buddhists sit in quiet meditation; Sufis whirl; Hindus offer sacrifices; Orthodox Jews bob their heads back and forth.

No matter what devotional mode of expression we use, God sees, hears and honors our homage to Him. When we express our divine love, we also nurture our spiritual growth.

Find your own way of demonstrating devotion. Ring bells, light candles or walk a labyrinth.

We can express our love for God in so many ways and He/She honors them all.

Affirmation: Today I revere God in my own individual style.

NAMASTE

November 2

Creative Wishing

"The wish is the father to the thought."
-William Shakespeare

Wishes are often the seeds of great inspiration. They start off as buds of desire and then reach their full bloom as realities.

Nurture your wish. Dance with it day-in-and-day-out until it blossoms into the reality of an unlimited possibility.

To quote, once again, our friend, Shakespeare, "I wish you all the joy that you can wish."

Affirmation: Wishing is the precursor to making my dream come true.

NAMASTE

November 3
We Are the Man in the Moon

"A tone of some world far from ours, where music and
moonlight and feeling are one."
-Percy Shelley

This evening, I'm sitting on my front porch, tape recorder in hand, staring up at a full moon in an indigo sky.

As I gaze at the glistening orb above me, I realize what strength it holds. Its gravitational pull is the reason for the ocean tides. It has even been used for the making of our calendars and many a baby has chosen to arrive on the night of a full moon.

Aren't we as human beings equally as amazing as the moon? Don't we contain the same Celestial Flame as our dear friend in the darkened sky?

We are the answer to all of life's mysteries, co-creators with the same Infinite Power that birthed that glowing satellite.

Affirmation: Like the moon, I am one of God's perfect creations.

NAMASTE

November 4
I Am Precious

"I saw my Lord with the eye of my heart, and I said:
Who art Thou? He said: Thou."
-Al Hallaj

How many of us realize how truly precious we are?

A dear, poet friend of mine wrote the following verse on just how vital we are to God.

I Am Precious

I am precious...
Like you,
A Jewel with dazzling facets.
Birthed by outbreath
Nourished through inbreath
As you,
One, yet all
Seen, though unseen
Sound, yet silence.
A flowing river of Love, unending
Like you,
I am (w)holy precious.
Arlene Hughes

Affirmation: I am precious.

NAMASTE

November 5
Polishing Our Souls

"Through forgiveness we polish our souls."
-Author

When my son, Mike, told me about a class he was taking, he said, "I took this course in order to shine my soul a little brighter."

I love that image!

As many of us have done, Michael is dealing with his past, coming to terms with how it impacted his life, and then forging on to forgiveness. Not an easy task, but an, oh, so important one.

Forgiving ourselves and others shines our souls a little brighter, causing a shift that miraculously changes our lives, allowing us to live in the magnificence of who we truly are.

Affirmation: Today I will practice forgiveness and let God show me a bigger universe.

NAMASTE

November 6

Setting Our Holiday Priorities

"He that always gives way to others will end in having
no principles of his own."

-Aesop

These next two months will be filled with holiday preparations and family gatherings. It is also a busier-than-usual time at our schools, workplaces and worship centers.

For most women, it is the season to take a deep breath and rethink our priorities.

What do you love most about these special days? Do you love baking, but dislike cooking the whole holiday meal? Maybe it's decorating that gets your creative juices flowing, but entertaining is right up there with a root canal. How many of you just want to curl up on the couch to read a good book or to watch "Miracle on Thirty-Fourth Street?"

Whatever your favorite holiday thing is, do it, and delegate the rest.

Affirmation: This year I will set holiday priorities.

NAMASTE

Open Wide Your Heart and Mind

"It is not from ego, but from Spirit that we truly create."
-Author

The more I write this book, the more I realize that it is not I who writes it, but, He.

In his book, Reclaim Your Spiritual Power, Ron Roth says, "Our most powerful and authentic inspiration originates from within us."

I might garner tremendously useful information from hearing inspirational speakers and reading the hundreds of spiritual books that line my shelves, but until I open myself to the creative flow of Spirit, I am a person of—no mind—no thought—no ideas.

Then, when I sit and ask the Beloved to open wide my heart and my mind, the thoughts and ideas flow like a gushing stream. Sometimes my hand cannot keep up with the words that pour forth and I find myself shaking with glee at the amazing and astonishing miracle of co-creation.

Affirmation: I open my heart and mind to God, and I create.

NAMASTE

November 8

Puttering in the Garden

"A morning-glory at my window satisfies me more than
the metaphysics of books."
-Walt Whitman

My step-daughter, Patti, taught us that here, in Southern California, November is the best time to plant sweet peas.

Every year, now, Bill and I sow our sweet pea seeds in the fall, and in the spring, we are always blessed with an abundance of bouquet-after-bouquet of those luscious smelling blooms.

Late October and early November are also the months to plant crocus, daffodils and tulips.

Spring is the time to reap the bounty of our autumn sowing. But fall is the season to pull on our gardening gloves and frolic in nature's playground.

Today, take yourself out to breakfast and then saunter through the nearest nursery to pick out your favorite seeds and bulbs. Become an "exterior" decorator, planning your color scheme with swatches of God's abundant natural materials.

Ralph Waldo Emerson wrote, "Earth laughs in flowers."

Affirmation: Today I will plant in order to have a spring full of laughter.

NAMASTE

November 9
Tearing Down Our Walls

"When we tear down the wall of separation, we then can
enjoy the dance of freedom."
-Author

Today we commemorate the anniversary of the fall of the Berlin Wall. On this day in 1989, the East German government proclaimed that East Berliners could enter West Berlin.

Masses of people scaled the huge barrier on that day and, over the weeks, thousands broke off fragments of the wall until the government eventually tore down the rest.

What is it in your life that, like that barricade, has separated you from others? Is it the lack of joy? A feeling of unworthiness? An unforgiving heart? Or perhaps it is the inability to feel thankful for even the smallest of blessings.

Like the people of Berlin on this day in 1989, start to chip away at your own personal bulwark of separation until you have torn it down completely.

Affirmation: Today I tear down my wall of separation.

NAMASTE

November 10
Living in the Present

"Now or never! You must live in the present, launch yourself on every wave, find eternity in the moment."
-Henry David Thoreau

Just as athletes center themselves to the absolute "now" while performing, we, too, should center our lives the same way—fully present.

Finding "eternity in the moment," as Mr. Thoreau suggests, is a wonderful way to live our lives, because each moment is indeed a very important part of our eternity.

I have spent the day writing this book and I certainly could not do that if I had been rehashing yesterday's events or worrying about tomorrow.

Our lives become more meaningful as we stay in the center of each unique and wonderful moment.

Affirmation: Today I will be aware of each and every present moment.

NAMASTE

November 11
The Songs of My Life

"Let the songs of our lives be an aria of love."
-Author

There is a gentle rain falling from the heavens this morning as Punkie and I sit on the front porch. The ground under the camphor trees is a sea of yellow, moist leaves, and, once again, the Eternal Poet whispers in my ear.

I want the songs of my life
To echo through the hills

To sing in the alleyways
And along the freeways
As ballads of both joy and sorrow.

To hum through gardens and forests
Like the golden-striped bees
And the soft-feathered birds.

I want the songs of my life
To hold the passionate nectar of sweetness
That I might fill all of humanity with love.
-Author

Affirmation: I make my life a living song.

NAMASTE

November 12
Wisdom

"Listen closely and you will find wisdom."
-Author

A dear friend discovered yesterday that sometimes wisdom comes from sources other than enlightened scribes.

Sandy went to our neighborhood department store to return a small case that was supposed to have a shoulder strap inside, but the strap seemed to be missing.

At the return counter, the clerk fished around inside the case and found the missing strap. Smiling, she said, "Sometimes when we look too hard for something, we just can't seem to find it."

This lovely woman's words gave Sandy something to "noodle" on for the rest of the day.

Sometimes, in our eagerness to find that "certain someone," or the "just right job," we need to quit looking and let our Heavenly Clerk do the fishing.

Affirmation: Wisdom comes from unusual places. I will listen carefully for it.

.

NAMASTE

November 13
Be Who You Are

"Your path, in any form, is divinity lived."
-Author

It is my path to write, to articulate on paper, the thoughts that float inside my head. Your expressive path may be something entirely different. If whatever you do makes you "happy," then you are living divinely.

Don't seek the path of another, trail blaze your own.

Akiba

When Akiba was on his deathbed, he bemoaned to his rabbi that he felt he was a failure. His rabbi moved closer and asked why, and Akiba confessed that he had not lived a life like Moses. The poor man began to cry, admitting that he feared God's judgment.

At this, his rabbi leaned into his ear and whispered gently, "God will not judge Akiba for not being Moses. God will judge Akiba for not being Akiba."

-From The Talmud

Affirmation: I will discover and live my own divinity.

NAMASTE

November 14
Competition

"Thou shalt not covet, but tradition approves all forms of competition."
-Arthur Clough

The sun is showing off this morning by intermittently popping its beaming orb through the attention-demanding clouds. I am fascinated by the act, waiting to see who will be center-stage next.

Like today's sun and clouds, the characteristic of being competitive is not a particularly bad one. We would not have football, tennis or any other sport, were it not for the love of competition.

Can we let go, however, of the need to have the most money, live in the most prestigious neighborhood, or have the largest collection of trophies?

Playing and living our games and our lives for the sheer joy of living and competing in an event will then make us less concerned about who wins or who has the most of anything. That way, not winning or winning won't impact our sense of adequacy or inadequacy.

It's how we choose to live our competitive nature that speaks to who we truly are.

I'm smiling, now, because, as I look up, Mr. Sol seems to be riding on Mr. Cloud's back.

Good teamwork, guys!

Affirmation: I can be lovingly competitive.

NAMASTE

November 15

Goodbye, Dear Friend

"Friendship is a sheltering tree.'
-Samuel Taylor Coleridge

I awaken to the sound of a chain saw. It is a shrill, raucous noise that sends shivers up my spine.

For now, my temporary bed is in the living room, because my injured back needs a hard surface on which to heal.

Outside my window, I see two men cutting down a large tree that had stood proudly on our greenbelt for more years than I have lived here.

For a month, I have communed with that tree, its strength and tenacity being an integral part of my healing. As limbs fall to the ground, I am witnessing the death of a very dear friend.

I call out to Bill to bring me a robe and help me down the stairs, then I limp over to the "crime-in-progress," holding up my hand for them to stop.

One of the men says, "Yes, ma'am, can we help you?"

With tears of grief, I ask if I can have a moment with the tree.

Glad, I suppose, to take a break, he answers, "Sure, lady, take your time."

My arms reach around this grand, old oak, and I whisper my thanks to him, tell him how much he has meant to me and that I will always remember him in love.

This happened four years ago and when I look out my window to where my friend once stood, I send a prayer of thanksgiving to a dear soul who, someday, I will hug once again.

Affirmation: I am soul-connected with all of nature.

NAMASTE

Ahhhh, Books!

"I cannot live without books."
-Thomas Jefferson

Here I am, sitting in my favorite bookstore, soaking up the music, gazing around at the books and magazines that surround me, knowing that I am in my element.

My romance with the written word started as a very young child when my mother would read to my sister and me. First it was Peter Rabbit, and Winnie the Pooh, and then, Mary Poppins, to name but a few.

I love that bookstores have changed over the years. Now they serve coffee, tea, sandwiches and every appealing dessert that might tickle your taste buds. Today I'm having chai tea and, of course, a chocolate brownie.

Many people love bar-hopping. My husband and I are happiest when we are bookstore-hopping. There is such peace in sitting at a table in the coffee-bar or in one of the "cushy" chairs placed here-and-there throughout the store.

Take yourself on a date to your favorite bookstore today. Relish the music, have a cup of tea and maybe something sinfully chocolate. Then carry home a book of poetry to remember your visit.

Affirmation: Today I treat myself to a bookstore.

NAMASTE

You as Fifty Fabulous Adjectives

"Who and how do I want to be in this world?"
-Author

Recently I ran across a page in my 2008 diary. It was entitled Me as Fifty Fabulous Adjectives.

I would like to share with you what I wrote. Some of these adjectives I already am and some I am still striving to be.

1. Friendly	26. Emotional
2. Happy	27. Aware
3. Talented	28. Exciting
4. Generous	29. Expressive
5. Beautiful	30. Wise
6. Vibrant	31. Colorful
7. Home loving	32. Stubborn
8. Creative	33. Compassionate
9. Blissful	34. Listening
10. Spiritual	35. Loyal
11. Ordinary	36. Enthusiastic
12. Extraordinary	37. Articulate
13. Peaceful	38. Engaging
14. Energetic	39. Irrepressible
15. Fun	40. Serious
16. Funny	41. Lovable
17. Cooperative	42. Organized

18. Outgoing	43. Present
19. Contemplative	44. Scared
20. Self-educated	45. Open
21. Dazzling	46. Discerning
22. Strong	47. Dreamer
23. Survivor	48. Miracle-worker
24. Loving	49. Spirit in a body
25. Sensitive	50. Wonderful

Sit down and write as many adjectives as you can think of that describe who you are, or who you want to be. You'll be surprised what comes up.

Affirmation: I am at least fifty fabulous adjectives.

NAMASTE

November 18

Living Out Loud

"If you ask me what I came into this world to do, I will tell you:
I came to live out loud."
-Emile Zola

I love the thought of living out loud, of throwing my arms up in the air and twirling around in circles. I want to sing at the top of my lungs that life is a soup pot full of zestful goodies just waiting to be tasted and relished!

We must usher in that "whoop it up" feeling every day, in celebration of just being alive!

Don't waste one minute of your life. Get out there and do what you came on this earth to do—live out loud!

Affirmation: Whatever living out loud means to me, I will do it!

NAMASTE

November 19

Our Divine Gifts

"There is no such thing as failure in co-creation."
-Author

Don't worry what your talents might be. Just pick up your pen, paintbrush or scroll saw and then step aside. The Infinite Creator will most assuredly take over from there.

We never create in a vacuum. Our talents are Divine gifts that promise us a magical journey of co-creation with God.

The Italian composer, Giacomo Puccini, said that his opera, Madame Butterfly, "was dictated to me by God; I was merely instrumental in putting it down on paper and communicating it to the public."

What gift has God given you? Be it cooking, sewing, painting, writing or music, just remember that, as you do it, you are co-creating with Spirit and so you cannot fail.

Affirmation: Today I will listen to the Great Co-Creator.

NAMASTE

November 20
Sharing

"Thousands of candles can be lighted from a single candle, and the life
of the candle will not be shortened.
Happiness never ceases by being shared.
-Buddha

As Thanksgiving approaches, we normally stop to ponder the many ways in which we have been blessed. Perhaps, this year, we can share that blessing by enhancing the lives of others.

In every city, there are shelters for the homeless, safe houses for women and their children, and soup kitchens for those in need of nourishment.

Take from your cupboard what excess you might have. Place it in a basket and deliver it to those who have a need for food.

Sharing our abundance is what Thanksgiving is all about.

Affirmation: I will share with others the plenty that God has shared with me.

NAMASTE

November 21
The Kitchen, Your Spiritual Center

"See the pot as your own head, and see the water as your life's blood."
-Zen Saying

The aromas wafting from my house and onto the front porch are tantalizing. Yes, Bill is cooking again.

Hurrah!

The smell of onions and garlic browning in olive oil are tempting me to put pad and pencil aside in order to help hurry along the epicurean delight of lentil soup.

Bill, having a strong Zen essence, brings that spiritual attribute into everything he does—especially cooking. Chopping becomes a meditation, an act of being present, of living in the now. Browning onions brings with it the sizzling of Spirit. The combining of various ingredients and their individual colors and flavors become the symbol of the blending of humanity and how we improve the taste of life by interacting with each other.

See your kitchen as a holy place where God and you create together.

Affirmation: My kitchen is my spiritual domain.

NAMASTE

Mother Nature

"Mother Earth is a Dynamic Woman."
-Patricia Price

Mother Nature is flawless in Her capacity to create both devastating havoc and delicate beauty.

She teaches us through earthquakes, tsunamis, and hurricanes that She is a powerful force. With plants, flowers and animal life, She exhibits Her softness and alluring charm.

From this Dynamic Woman we learn the experience of her shadow side and rejoice in the times of Her light and excellence.

We dance on the ballroom of Her glades and mourn before Her crypts of sorrow.

She is the artist of the stripes on a zebra, the round, black spots on the ladybug and the autumnal colors of fall.

Mother Nature fuses heaven and earth into a temple of four seasons where blessings and cursings alike fall upon us like petals from a Divine Mother Tree.

Through it all, She imparts to us the explosive lessons of suffering, love, humbleness and humility.

The Mistress of the Universe knows when to realign, when to bring forth beauty and when to rest.

Affirmation: I honor the dynamic feminine of Mother Nature.

NAMASTE

November 23

Enjoy the Morning

"Do not shorten the morning by getting up late; look upon it as the quintessence of life, as to a certain extent sacred."
-Arthur Schopenhauer

Morning is a hallowed time for me. I lie with eyes closed, silently repeating my daily affirmations. Then, I turn to my Buddhist Metta Loving Kindness practice.

I dip into the well of my day, bringing up a pail full of ideas for my book. My imagination conjures up a piece of French toast covered with juicy, ripe strawberries. Then, after breakfast, I look forward to the caress of a warm shower on my body.

Throwing back the covers, I leave the shelter of my bed and begin the sacred ritual of my day.

"She waits the dawn, so eager to be born,
Yearning to press her bosom to the sun,
To meet the day that dewdrops adorn,
Mingling
Till at last they are one."
-Arlene Hughes

Affirmation: I greet the sacredness of morning.

NAMASTE

Giving Thanks

"If the only prayer you said in your whole life was
thank you—that would suffice."
-Meister Eckhart

This is the month of Thanksgiving, the month when families gather around the dining room table—a table set with grandma's finest china and crystal. It is a glorious time of eating too much turkey and stuffing, in a room full of laughing and loving.

We have so very much to be thankful for on a daily basis: our homes that shelter and protect us, our loved ones who help make us who we are, the family pet, that unconditionally loving piece of fur who entertains us with his antics and expressions and, most importantly, we have the life that God has given us in order that we might fulfill our purpose here on this beautiful earth.

The Common Book of Prayer, says it all so eloquently, "Let us come before His presence with thanksgiving; and show ourselves glad in Him with psalms."

Affirmation: I am thankful for everything and everyone in my life.

NAMASTE

November 25
Fulfilling Our Intentions

"Pray devoutly, hammer stoutly."
-English Proverb

We can pray five times a day to be an award-winning author or artist, but unless we write our books and paint our pictures, our prayers can't possibly be answered.

At one point in my life, I asked God for financial abundance and then continued using my credit cards until I found myself knee-deep in debt. When I finally woke up and quit using those little plastic deceivers, I paid off my debt and now carry one card in case of an emergency or to scrape the ice off of my windshield.

We can set all the intentions we want, but unless we "hammer stoutly," those intentions will be useless.

Affirmation: I set my intentions and hammer stoutly.

NAMASTE

November 26

Altruism

"Developing an altruistic heart can only lead to peace."
-Author

Our world would certainly change and flourish if each person would take a "vow of altruism." If each of us could sign a contract that we would unselfishly show concern and love to every sentient being on earth, we would, for the first time, have an end to war.

Affirmation: I will strive to be altruistic.

NAMASTE

November 27

Autumn Leaves

"November's sky is chill and drear,
November's leaf is red and sear."
-Sir Walter Scott

Falling leaves remind us that our lives, once green and fresh, will all too soon wither on the branch of life and die.

It is while clinging to the limb that we are alive, dancing in the wind, protecting the fruit of mankind and shading the human race from the withering sun of hate and hypocrisy.

Let us use our tree-time to rejoice in the life that we have been given, to flutter in the breeze of existence and to wrap mankind in our protective, vibrant leaves.

Affirmation: I will use my tree time wisely.

NAMASTE

November 28

Compassion

"Compassion is God expressing Himself through us."
-Author

Compassion denotes tenderheartedness, gentleness, caring, concern and benevolence. It means reaching out to another person, a distressed animal or even a helpless tree about to be destroyed. We also need to express this same gentleness toward ourselves.

When we express compassion, our hearts respond to another's hurt and we can feel the same love of God surging through us.

Affirmation: Today I embrace compassion.

NAMASTE

November 29
Enduring Love

"How do I love thee, let me count the ways."
-Elizabeth Barrett Browning

Bill and I married twenty-five years ago today. We were both in our fifty's, both ready for that Elizabeth and Robert Browning relationship. In each other, we found it.

Like gardeners, Bill and I have tended to our marriage, weeding out the tendrils of unkind, useless words and deeds. To keep our love blooming, we have fed the blossoms of our relationship with quiet understanding, gentle patience and the ability to be "spiritual gurus" to each other.

I would like to share with you an Arabian proverb about friendship that also reaches out to touch our married lives: "A friend is one to whom one may pour out all the contents of one's heart, chaff and grain together, knowing that the gentlest of hands will take and sift it, keep what is worth keeping, and with a breath of kindness blow the rest away."

Happy anniversary, my beloved Zen Man!

Affirmation: I will weed out the unkind, useless words and deeds, allowing my marriage to blossom.

NAMASTE

November 30

Flowing

"Flowing water does not decay."
-Chinese Proverb

When you don't resist the flow of your life, you move through your days more easily. Stopping the flow stagnates the water. Trying to change the flow causes the water to become turbulent.

See yourself stepping into your kayak and letting the river of your life's possibility and purpose take you where it will.

Affirmation: I will let the river of life take me toward my destination.

NAMASTE

December 1

Evening

"This is a delicious evening, when the whole body is one sense, and imbibes delight through every pore."
-Henry David Thoreau

Tonight, I view the image of a "delicious evening" in the radiance of the moon's brilliance shining on the water of our pond.

There is so much beauty in the dark silhouettes of the trees outside my window, in the chill of December's frosty entrance and the screech of a night owl's song.

The hours spent writing have left me spiritually fulfilled, yet languid and inert.

A day well spent is its own reward and now I rest.

Affirmation: I will enjoy my delicious evenings.

NAMASTE

December 2
A Child's Best Friend

"Dreams, books, are each a world; and books, we know, are
a substantial world, both pure and good."
-William Wordsworth

Martin Tupper wrote, "A good book is the best of friends, the same today and forever."

How right he was!

My four-year-old great-granddaughter will not go to sleep at night until her bed is full of books. It's not the stuffed animals she craves, it's her books.

What more valuable gift is there to give a child than a gift of the written word? I have books from my youth that I cherish more than any of the other works in my library.

Nurture your young one's inherent love for reading by lavishing them with a variety of books this Christmas. Give them the gift of reading.

Affirmation: I will put books on my Christmas list.

NAMASTE

December 3

You

"Who is the you that is you?"
-Author

Do you know what a miracle you are; that in this world there is not a soul quite like you?

You are a unique blend of "perfect," and, sometimes, "not so perfect." It is your ultimate choice to be either one.

I like to think of the word "you" as an acronym:

Y our

O wn

U nderstanding

How do you understand yourself to be? How do you perceive yourself? Of what desires and ambitions are you aware?

Set aside today to have a date with that person called "You," and get to know who "You" truly are. Recognize that unique child of God that rests within your body and your mind.

Meister Eckhart wrote, "Become aware of what is in you. Announce it, pronounce it, produce it and give birth to it."

Affirmation: Today I will get to know the you that is me.

NAMASTE

December 4

Connecting With Love

"An amazing life requires connection."
-Loretta LaRoche
Life Is Short—Wear Your Party Pants

When Bill and I lived in Pismo Beach, we often ate at one especially good Italian restaurant. *Rosa's* was named for its owner and she made it a habit to walk from table-to-table, greeting all of us as though we were part of her large, Italian family.

I was listening to a local cooking show on the radio one Saturday morning and they announced that there would be a buffet at another nearby restaurant, and that there would be a contest for the three best potato salads. "Bring your favorite recipe and possibly win a prize," they said.

I'd never entered a cooking contest in my life, but it sounded like fun. So, I grabbed my cookbook and started immediately to concoct a hot German potato salad.

When Bill and I entered the restaurant where the contest was being held, we noticed that Mama Rosa was sitting with her family at one of the tables. Later, we discovered that her son was one of the tasting judges.

We enjoyed a lovely buffet and then the cooking show lady announced it was time to judge the many potato salads the contestants had brought, that day.

First place went to a woman whose salad came from a long-time family recipe. Second place was awarded to a woman who had gotten her formula from her great-aunt.

When they announced that Molly Dillon was the third-place winner, I thought, "Oh, dear John! Do I lie and say it was Great Grandma Tillman's recipe or do I tell the truth?

Hesitantly, I took the microphone in my hand and said, "Betty Crocker is not exactly a blood relative, although she's been a family member for years, so we got together this morning and made this salad."

Laughter accompanied me back to my seat, but before I could get there, Rosa hurried over, pinched both of my cheeks, and said, in her beautiful accent, "I just love you!"

Wow! Did I connect with love! That one cheek-pinching incident meant more to me than that precious woman will ever know. I truly connected with her amazing love.

Affirmation: Today I find ways to connect with love.

NAMASTE

December 5

Learning From Adversity

"Sweet are the uses of adversity."
-William Shakespeare

I believe that all of the pain and adversity in the universe has a purpose.

In the Bible, we read how a blind man was brought to Jesus. The one who brought him, asked the Master, "Rabbi, who sinned, this man or his parents, that he was born blind?"

Jesus replied, "It was not that this man sinned, nor his parents, but that the works of God might be manifest in him."

We are asked not to seek the reason for our adversity, but rather to discover the lessons that suffering always brings with it.

Our hardships are no one's fault; they are merely circumstances that cause us to reflect, even in our pain, on the grace and the love of Spirit. Perhaps it is just a time to, "Be still and know that I am God."

Affirmation: I will find peace in my adversity.

NAMASTE

December 6
Divine Potential

"You have potential beyond measure in a universe of
countless possibilities."
-Patricia Price

Look up the word "potential" in the dictionary and you will find that
it means "capable of being or becoming" and "a latent excellence or
ability that may or may not be developed."

Similarly, I like to think of "divine potential" as being that untapped
ability to attain our highest good.

When we open ourselves to our deepest longing and take steps
toward achieving our goals, we may first need to move past our fears—
past the belief that we might fail. The truth is that with the help and
guidance of the Infinite Achiever, we are capable of co-creation on all
levels.

We simply open up to the presence and potency of God and let the
magic begin!

My daughter, Debbie, has a passion for teaching. At the age of
forty-five, she decided to complete her college education in order to
become a special education teacher. She then furthered her education
by earning a master's degree.

This is someone, who, at the age of eighteen months, nearly died of spinal meningitis. Her doctor informed me that if she did live, the extreme brain damage caused by the disease would leave her in a vegetative state.

Well, my precious "carrot" beat the odds, and realizing her "divine potential" has gone on to achieve her "highest good."

What would you do if you knew you could not fail?

DO IT!

Affirmation: By co-creating with God, I achieve my highest good.

NAMASTE

December 7

Stepping Toward God

"If you take one step in God's direction, He will take
ten steps toward you."
-Old Mystic Saying

Every single one of us was born with Divinity intact. It is the God-essence that allows us to receive guidance directly from Spirit.

It is sad that, along the way, through our misled "educations," we have lost sight of that Divine Intelligence. We have lost confidence in God and in our God-selves.

When our eyes are set only on the material world, we let go of our true essence—of our divinity.

As we wander away from our True North, we lose our way, our love, our peace and the ability to receive guidance from the Almighty Compass.

Like the prodigal son, we need to return to the Father.

Affirmation: Today I will take one step in God's direction.

NAMASTE

December 8

Sixty-Minute Friendships

"We cannot tell the precise moment when friendship is formed."
-James Boswell

My friend, Linda, and I were browsing through our local bookstore when she pointed out to me a book entitled, Transitions. Linda was saying that the book was so helpful for those going through difficult changes in their lives.

As my friend and I continued to talk, a lovely woman approached us saying, "Excuse me, I couldn't help but overhear you." She then went on to tell us about the changes that had transpired in her life: the death of her husband; her recent move to our town; and a son, who was undergoing dialysis and had moved back home so she could help care for him.

Linda and I invited Pattie to sit with us and have tea. For an hour we talked, getting to know each other better.

When we parted, we exchanged cards, hugs and a mutual feeling of having experienced a beautiful sixty-minute-friendship.

Affirmation: I will look for the opportunity of a sixty-minute friendship.

NAMASTE

December 9
Break Out the Decorations

"At Christmas play and make good cheer, for Christmas
comes but once a year."
-Thomas Tusser

It is time to break out the treasured decorations that are so much a part of our holiday traditions.

Set up the Christmas tree and lovingly handle each ornament, thinking back to the time it was purchased and the reason it hangs on your tree, year-after-year.

Be sure to play your favorite Christmas music to enhance the mood while you trim your tree. No matter how many times we have heard "Jingle Bells" or "Silent Night," those songs never fail to pull at our holiday heart strings.

Let the Holidays begin!

Affirmation: Today I will light a candle and decorate my tree.

NAMASTE

December 10
To What Spiritual Path are You Called?

"We are each on a unique, perfect spiritual journey."
-Author

It is often a "puzzlement" to some that there are many paths leading to the same Awesome Oneness. I have spoken of this before but feel it bears repeating.

I am blessed to attend a Spiritual Center that accepts all faiths. It is such a freeing experience to realize that God is the thread that holds each individual belief—each religion—each precious pearl.

As Reverend Margaret Stortz writes in the March, 2009, issue of The Science of Mind Magazine, "In some ways, this spiritual walk can be somewhat daunting. Some of the Arthurian tales have said that when the Knights of the Roundtable sought the Holy Grail, they could not follow one another's path because it rolled up behind them as they went forward—a sweet metaphor for suggesting that we must ultimately walk our own paths and not another's."

Affirmation: My spiritual path is perfect for me.

NAMASTE

December 11
A Joyous Season—or Not

"Happiness is a perfume you cannot pour on others without
getting a few drops on yourself."
-Ralph Waldo Emerson

For most of us, the holidays are times of family gatherings, parties and wonderful memories of past Christmases.

But not for all of us.

For some, the memories from childhood scream out anger and abuse. It has left us with a feeling of abandonment, which always seems to heighten around the holidays.

Our times of youth are the foundations for the rest of our lives. Unless and until we deal with those memories, they will, like Scrooge's ghosts, continue to haunt us.

May I suggest that, you, with less than happy recollections of Christmas, give yourselves the gift of a loving therapist?

Or it might be cathartic to make up a happy childhood by writing a fictional autobiography about your past joyful family holidays. Think of all the things that you wanted to happen in your life when you were young. Rewrite your past and, who knows, you might end up with a best-selling novel or a TV sitcom.

Another healing vehicle that you can use is to visit shut-ins or take gifts to those in assisted care who never have visitors.

Sprinkle a little happiness on others and you'll find you can't help but benefit from those residual drops.

Affirmation: This Christmas I will release my past and enjoy the holidays.

NAMASTE

December 12
Let it Go

"Finish every day and be done with it. You have done what you could. Some blunders and absurdities no doubt creep in; forget them as soon as you can."
-Ralph Waldo Emerson

Whatever errors, failures or worries that might be plaguing you—let them go!

You can't "rerun" your life's tape and start over, so bless the past and forgive it.

My grandmother loved her family and was also a huge worrier. She would call several times a day if one of us was ill to find out how we were doing.

My dad once said, "Ma, why don't you go sit in a corner and just worry for an hour. Get it all out of your system!"

Not a bad idea. Better yet, go see a funny movie and buy one of those HUGE boxes of popcorn.

Affirmation: No matter what I do or say, God loves me unconditionally and wants me to have a HUGE box of popcorn.

NAMASTE

December 13
Accomplishing the Impossible

"When God is doing something wonderful He begins with a difficulty.
But when He is going to do something very wonderful
He begins with an impossibility."
-Anonymous

Like Don Quixote, how many of us want to dream the impossible dream? We have undertaken a challenge that could very well become one of the greatest experiences of our lives.

Maybe our dream is to climb Mount Everest, write a book or start our own business.

As we undertake our dream, we need always to remember that God is able to do something very wonderful in our supposed impossibility.

Affirmation: I will dream and do the impossible.

NAMASTE

December 14
God is Our Only Source

"Step into the mind of God and let go of a consciousness of lack."
-Author

God is our only source of everything. All of our wealth comes through the Infinite Giver, not through our inheritances, our investments, nor our financial institutions, not even our employers.

ONLY GOD!

Most of the time when we receive an inheritance, it isn't long before we've spent it all. And, even when we invest it, a recession can hit with such force that our investments become all but worthless. Look what happened to the banks in 2009! And in that same year unemployment hit an all-time high.

We need to step into the mind of God and totally release the idea of lack! Whatever we think becomes our truth. If we continually speak of "not having enough," then that is exactly how much we will have.

If, however, we thank God for what we have, use our time and our money wisely, feeling daily the excitement and joy of the prosperity and abundance that is our rightful inheritance from our Heavenly Father, then that is exactly what our experience will be—no need for "bailouts!"

The only thing required is the understanding that our source of everything is not based on the material, but is merely a reflection of our beliefs.

Affirmation: God is my only source.

NAMASTE

December 15
Winter Celebrations

"Namaste—the divine in me greets the divine in you."
-Sanskrit Greeting

Winter brings with it many celebrations, all derived from festivities of the solstice—the return of the light, of the lengthening days.

Hanukah, Christmas, Kwanza and the Hindu Festival of Lights will all be celebrated this month.

At our spiritual center, we observe all of these traditions. How exciting it is to honor our shared faiths. Every year, we enjoy the delicious foods connected to each particular spiritual precept. We play the music and sing the chants and songs connected with these celebrations.

This month, teach your children about the many celebrations of winter. Cook the foods, listen to the music and quote the prayers together from each faith.

Bring the light of peace, love and interfaith into your home.

Affirmation: This year I will observe all the winter ceremonies.

NAMASTE

December 16

Friendships

"Gratefulness waters old friendships and makes new ones sprout."
-Russian Proverb

Perhaps today would be the perfect time to brew a pot of tea, turn up the Christmas music and write your holiday greetings.

Each year, right after Christmas, Bill and I make a luncheon date and, together, choose our cards for the next year.

I love sorting through the colorful boxes, reading the messages and picking the perfect cards. As I write notes inside each one, I thank God for each of my friends and family, watering that relationship whether old or new.

Affirmation: Today I will write Christmas cards and water my friendships.

NAMASTE

December 17
The Gift of Love

"I think I could turn and live with animals, they are so
placid and self-contained."
-Walt Whitman

When we think of gift-giving, our image is that of a present attractively wrapped and sitting under the Christmas tree.

One of my favorite gifts was given to me by a neighbor. We named her "Punkie." That three-pound ball of love is the dearest thing I own—the best present I've ever received.

If you are willing to make the commitment, and take on the responsibility of caring for a pet, then visit a nearby animal shelter this holiday season and carefully choose a cat or a dog for yourself or a loved one.

A lonely animal will receive the blessing of a home and you will know the joy of an unconditionally loving companion.

Affirmation: Merry Christmas to me, or maybe, to Grandma.

NAMASTE

December 18

Dream it Into Being

"Kick out the critic in your head and soar!"
-Author

I was drinking a cup of tea in the coffee shop of a local bookstore, when I noticed a group of people sitting around a nearby table. They were reading aloud and then critiquing each other's work.

I scooted my chair closer so that I could hear what they were saying. The leader noticed my interest and invited me to join them.

At the end of the critiquing session, paper and pencils were passed around and the woman-in-charge asked if I would like to join them in a quick writing assignment. I agreed, thinking it might be fun.

Each of us then shared what we had written, and when I read mine, the leader asked, "How long have you been writing?"

I looked at my watch and replied, "About fifteen minutes."

This happened ten years ago. I went home that day with the determination to write. Then, one morning, following my experience with the critique group, I woke up with an entire plot for a novel racing through my mind.

Were there times when I threw pages across the room in frustration? YES!

Were there moments in writing the book when I just didn't think I could do it?

YES!

Did I find a million reasons for not sitting down to write, like cleaning the garage or the entire house?

YES! YES! YES!

But, I did it anyway and now my book, Margo, is a published work.

Whatever it is you want in life, plow through, shift your perception, kick out the critic in your head and soar!

Affirmation: I can do whatever I want by dreaming it into being and giving up my reasons and excuses why I can't.

NAMASTE

December 19
The Beauty of the Season

"A heart in love with beauty never grows old."
-Turkish Proverb

Bill and I drove around tonight looking at the houses in our town—homes abundantly decorated with Christmas lights and holiday scenes.

I always feel like a little kid again when we take our yearly jaunt around the city. The magic and splendor of the season comes alive with the animated characters and brilliant lights.

Busy sidewalks of people strolling along, singing Christmas carols, stop now and then to greet each other, touching the happy child within.

At the end of our trek, the cocoa at our nearby coffee shop completes our perfect evening.

Affirmation: The beauty of the season will include Christmas lights and cocoa.

NAMASTE

December 20
What Gifts Can We Give to Ourselves?

"God gives us the gift of life and, to that, we add our own offerings."
-Author

This is the month for the giving and receiving of gifts. Today, I would like you to imagine that under your Christmas tree, there are many colorfully-wrapped presents, and on every box is a tag with your name written on it.

Now take this whimsical vision even further and recognize that you are both the giver and the recipient of these beautifully packaged offerings.

What lies within each of these carefully chosen, delightful gifts? What have you handpicked for yourself?

Allow me to open my own gifts and share with you my most prized possessions; the gifts of:

~ Silence for meditation and prayer

~ Seeing, in order that I might read and enjoy the beauty of nature

~ Taking my daily chores and turning them into sacred rituals

~ A Spiritual Center where I can gather with like-minded loved ones to worship, learn and play

~ My husband, children and other family members who complete me so wondrously

~Friends and strangers who filter in and out of my life, teaching me unconditional love

~ The Beloved, that Living Spiritual Passion within me

~ The talents of singing, writing, crocheting and cooking that give my days meaning and substance

And, as I open the last gift, there bursts forth more love than can be contained in one lifetime, much less one box. Love acquired through forgiveness, through a passion and joy for life, through seventy-five years of Spiritual and emotional growth and through time spent with Infinite Love.

I would like for you to contemplate your own imaginary gifts, opening them carefully one-by-one. I believe that every offering might well differ for each of us depending on our age, our circumstances and our various Spiritual paths.

As you unwrap each present, write it down on a piece of paper. Save that list in a "precious place," and ten years from now, again open more gifts and see how your thoughts and offerings might have changed.

Affirmation: My life is blessed with gifts that I allow myself to open.

NAMASTE

December 21
Today We Celebrate the Winter Sosltice.

"May the lights of Winter Solstice illuminate your life."
-Author

Each year, on December 21, Winter Solstice rituals have been held in practically every culture. India, Africa, Scandinavia, Persia, North and South America, Britain and China all celebrate the Solstice.

Since light is the general, unifying theme, the celebration often uses the substance of fire. Bonfires, Yule logs, and candles are used in the various ceremonies.

Today, celebrate the Winter Solstice by lighting a special candle. Let the brightness of that candle be a beacon of God's blessing for your home and out into the universe, symbolizing peace and love.

Affirmation: I will light a Solstice candle.

NAMASTE

December 22

Cookies—Cookies—Cookies!

"Cookies are God's 'Tidings of Comfort and Joy.'"
-Author

Two years ago, suffering yet another bout of insanity, Bill and I decided we would break all cookie-baking records.

Each morning for weeks before Christmas, we took three or four recipes, baked all day and then counted and froze our offerings.

Shortly before Santa's arrival, we had tallied up and filled three freezers with over 6,000 homemade cookies. The night we finished our marathon baking, we high-fived each other and dropped into bed, with visions of sugar plums, and cookie dough, dancing in our heads.

What is the holiday season without chocolate chip, snickerdoodle or gingerbread goodies?

Put on your creative cookie cap and bake up a batch, of your favorite, sweet culinary delights.

Call me when they're done. I'll be right over!

Affirmation: Today I bake. Tomorrow I stay off of the scales.

NAMASTE

December 23

What Can We Give Our Children?

"A rich child often sits in a poor mother's lap."
-Danish Proverb

As parents, we sometimes feel that "Santa Claus" will be diminished in our children's eyes if we don't lavish them with expensive gifts and toys.

Is that what our youngsters really want? Oh, they think they do, but how many times has the playhouse been shoved aside in order for the huge box it came in to become a fort?

Unconditional love, listening to our children, and respecting their individual personalities doesn't cost a dime. Those are the gifts that build character.

Today, take some of those cookies that you baked yesterday, join your little ones in icing those that need frosting, and have a pre-Christmas party.

Affirmation: Today I will love my children with a cookie party.

NAMASTE

December 24
A Christmas Outing

"Perhaps the best yuletide decoration is being wreathed in smiles."
-Author Unknown

Today is Christmas Eve, a time of family love, mistletoe and waiting with bated breath for Santa to arrive.

I would like to share with you a story that I have written in honor of the season:

The voices of the excited group rang out in unison for the annual holiday countdown: ten-nine-eight-seven-six-five-four-three-two-ONE! A roar swelled up from the throng of happy spectators as the imposing Christmas tree in Rockefeller Center lit up with a million, glittering, bright-colored lights.

Almost immediately after the lighting, the masses began separating, some to get a closer look at the grand spectacle and some to stroll through gaily decorated shops or over to the nearest coffee house.

Suzie stood gazing silently at the sparkling magnificence before her. It had become an annual tradition for her to enjoy the lighting of the holiday tree and mingle with the crowd. "It just wouldn't be Christmas without this event," she noted to herself. "Now comes the best part of all." Her golden, silky hair bounced as she trotted along the sidewalk. Nearing the corner restaurant and coffee house, her pace slowed considerably as she breathed in the luscious aromas wafting from each doorway.

Content and a little tired after her escapade, she turned and strolled back toward her uptown apartment, stopping briefly to enjoy the carolers dressed in their Victorian period costumes. The women wore lovely bonnets and heavy velveteen dresses of deep maroon and moss green. The men were elegant in their top hats, striped pants and tails. What a fantastic musical ending to a perfect evening. Suzie shivered slightly from the cold air and scurried on her way.

It was a welcoming sight, as she rounded the corner, to see Jake, the doorman. He stood in front of the Fifth Avenue high-rise apartment, holding the large glass-and- chrome door open for her.

"My goodness, Miss Suzie," he shouted, "Get in here before you catch your death of cold."

Suzie ran into the warmth of the elegant lobby and up the plush, carpeted staircase.

The doorman smiled broadly muttering to himself, "How many years has that cute little cocker spaniel made the trek out on this same night? Must be about eight now. If her mistress had the slightest idea that I let her go anywhere by herself, she'd have my head on a platter! Oh well, Merry Christmas, my furry little friend."

And a very merry Christmas Eve to you all!

Affirmation: I will spread love and joy to the world.

NAMASTE

December 25
Merry Christmas!

"It's Christmas Day! Thank God I haven't missed it!"
-Charles Dickens

I woke up this morning to the smell of celery and onions sizzling in a pan—stuffing material for the turkey!

Bill was in the kitchen and Christmas carols floated in the same air as the savory aromas.

Languishing in bed, I thought back on all of the Christmases of my past: Grandma's chaotic holidays with cousins running about through the house; Aunt Mae hiding my olive pits in her napkin so my parents wouldn't know how many olives I had eaten; waking up at an ungodly hour to see what Santa had delivered; my children's sparkling eyes on Christmas morning.

Today, another memory-making holiday stretched before me and I thought of Mr. Dickens's words, "Oh, would that Christmas lasted the whole year through as it ought . . . Would that the spirit of Christmas could live within our hearts every day of the year."

Affirmation: God bless us everyone!

NAMASTE

December 26
Loving the Divine

"If you wish to know the Divine, feel the wind on your
face and the warm sun on your hand."
-Buddha

Today, see the world through the moon-struck eyes of a lover.

Embrace the joy of simply walking on this planet. Take pleasure in the caress of a gentle snow flake or a beam from the sun as it kisses your uplifted face.

Be here.

Be now.

Be love.

Affirmation: My lover is the Universe.

NAMASTE

December 27
Music, Maestro, Please

"And the night shall be filled with music, and the cares, that infest the day, shall fold their tents, like the Arabs, and as silently steal away."
-Henry Wadsworth Longfellow

Music fills our minds with memories from the past. It transports us back into times, both happy and sad, touching our souls in an intimate way.

As we close our eyes and listen to Beethoven, Bach or the Beatles, we are carried to a place of sheer feeling.

Music cannot be seen nor does an orchestrated sonata have words, yet the crescendo of a magnificently written piece can bring us to our knees.

Nature, too, has her own music. We hear in a brook, the rippling tones of water. The song of the wind often lulls us to sleep. The rain taps a syncopated rhythm against our windowpane, and, in the crash of a wave against a cliff, we experience the end of a great concerto.

Music reaches within us, interlocking our souls with the Divine.

Shakespeare wrote, "How sweet the moonlight sleeps upon this bank! Here we will sit, and let the sounds of music creep in our ears: soft stillness and the night becomes the touches of sweet harmony."

Affirmation: Music fills my day.

NAMASTE

December 28
A Comforting Box of Memories

"Oft in the stilly night,
Ere slumber's chain has bound me,
Of other days around me."
-Clement Clarke Moore

On the top shelf of my closet, I keep what I call my "Precious Box." In it, I place objects that mean something to me—touch my heart.

This colorful box contains such things as special cards, letters that, my grandchildren and other family members have written, and an envelope of foreign paper currency that my son's friend gave me, saying, "In case you need it on your travels."

Those and other trinkets afford me great joy every time I take that brightly colored receptacle down from the closet to pause and remember.

It might even be called my "Serenity Box." Often, when I feel like screaming, "Stop the world, I want to get off," I take it to my sanctuary and spend the afternoon reading my cards and letters and dream of traveling to far-off places, where I will spend my foreign money.

Today, go on a shopping quest and pick out a lovely box or basket. Then start gathering memories that will get you through those "less than happy" moments of your life.

Affirmation: Today I will start a "Precious Box" of memories.

NAMASTE

December 29
The Power of Love

"The property of power is to protect."
-Blaise Pascal

What is power? Is it just something we use to force people into submission?

What about the strength of love?

We can all offer a winning smile, a vigorous hug, a potent compliment, or, perhaps, help to empower others when they are down. These and other kindnesses are the real attributes of a truly powerful person.

William Gladstone wrote, "We look forward to the time when the power of love will replace the love of power. Then will our world know the blessings of peace."

Affirmation: I am lovingly powerful.

NAMASTE

December 30
A Gratitude Ceremony

"The sweet taste of gratitude lingers on my tongue."
-Author

A friend of mine recently shared a beautiful, yummy, and, yes, chocolaty way she and her husband have of expressing their gratitude.

Periodically, they brew a pot of fragrant jasmine tea and place a large bowl of Hershey Kisses in the center of their kitchen table.

Taking turns, they reach into the bowl, take out a brightly wrapped kiss and say what they are thankful for. Then they pop the candy into their mouth.

What sweet morsels their blessings become when they savor the taste of thankfulness.

Affirmation: Today, I will taste the sweetness of gratitude with someone I love.

NAMASTE

December 31

Reflections

"Should auld acquaintance be forgot
And never brought to mind?
Should auld acquaintance be forgot
And days of auld lang syne!"
-Robert Burns

As the year comes to a close, let us reflect on the myriad adventures that have been ours in that 365-day period—the dark times of growth through tribulation and the dazzling periods of joy and pleasure.

Throughout each day, the Infinite Keeper of Moments has walked beside us, sometimes even picking us up and carrying us when to keep trudging seemed an impossible chore.

May I encourage you to stop and reflect on the many blessings of the past year and to envision the countless number of sacred moments that stretch before you in the year ahead.

Prayer for the New Year
May peace fill all the empty spaces around you and in you.
May contentment answer all your wishes.
May comfort be yours, warm and soft like a sigh.
And may the coming year show you that every day is really a first day, a new year.
Let abundance be your constant companion, so that you have much to share.
May mirth be near you always, like a lamp shining brightly on

the many paths you travel.

May you be true love.

-Author Unknown

Affirmation: I bless and release the old year and look forward, with joy, to the new year.

NAMASTE

About the Author

After spending sixty-five years being an avid reader of every spiritual, metaphysical and fictional work she could get her hands on, Molly Dillon decided it was time to write her own books.

So, upon her retirement from thirty years as an executive secretary, she took pen in hand and started writing.

In addition to *Welcome to My Front Porch*, she is the author of *Margo*, the first of a series of Blue Harbor novels. The second in the series will be released in 2013.

Molly lives in Corona, California, with her husband, Bill.

Made in the USA
Charleston, SC
06 December 2012